Balanced Approach를 활용한 21세기

초등영어 지도방법

함정현 · 오현주

태영출판사

For Kenny, Jenny, Annie

Preface

초등영어를 펴내며

– We learn –

10% of what we read
20% of what we hear
30% of what we see
50% of what we both see and hear
70% of what is discussed with others
80% of what we experience personally
95% of what we teach someone else

by William Glasser

Willam Glasser가 말할 것처럼 무언가를 읽으면서 10%를 배우게 되고, 들으면서 20%를, 보면서 30%를, 보고 들으면서 50%를, 다른 사람과 토론을 하면서 70%를, 개인적으로 경험을 하면서 80%를, 그리고 다른 사람을 가르치면서 우리는 95%를 배우게 된다. 여기에 하나 더 나의 경험을 추가해서 말한다면 책을 집필하면서 더욱 많이 배우게 되었다.

이 책을 쓴 이유는 시중에 나와 있는 영어교재를 보면서 많은 아쉬움을 느꼈기 때문이다. 이 책에 제시된 이론과 방법을 차근차근 익혀나간다면 우리 아이들은 영어에 흥미를 갖고 쉽고 재미있게 영어를 배울 수 있을 것이다. 이 책은 'Balanced Literacy Approach' 에 의한 영어지도 방법을 제시하였고, 영어교육에 종사하고 있거나 이에 관심을 두고 공부하는 사람들을 위해 집필하였다. 또한 앞으로 우리의 영어교육이 어떤 방향으로 가야 할지, 어떻게 지도해야 효과적일지 연구하는 사람들에게 지침이 될 수 있도록 되도록 자세한 설명과 예시를 들어 구성하였다. 이 책을 꾸준히 읽고 익힌다면 초등 영어교육에 관심을 가진 모든 사람에게 든든한 안내자가 될 수 있을 것이라 믿는다.

끝으로, 이 책을 출판하는데 자료를 수집해 준 영재교육계발연구소 연구원들, 책이 나오기까지 시간과 노력을 아까지 않은 태영출판사 편집인 여러분, 이 책의 출판을 위해 너무나 고생하신 오현주 선생님, 그리고 항상 뒤에서 큰 힘이 되어 주시는 부모님께 깊이 감사드린다.

2009. 1. 5

저자 대표 함 정 현

C • O • N • T • E • N • T • S

Part Ⅰ. 21세기 영어교육의 방향

C • O • N • T • E • N • T • S

Part Ⅱ. 읽기(Reading)란 무엇인가?

Part Ⅲ. 쓰기(Writing)란 무엇인가?

Part Ⅰ
21세기 영어교육의 방향

1) 미국 교육계의 동향
2) 읽기, 쓰기를 강조하는 이유
3) 파닉스 접근법(Phonics Approach)
4) 총체적 언어 접근법(Whole Language Approach)
5) 균형잡힌 접근법(Balanced Literacy Approach)

79세 미국인 할아버지가 독일의 숲 속에서 길을 잃고 헤매다가 현지 주민에게 발견되어 구조 되었다. 이 때 할아버지가 지니고 있던 지도는 1차 대전 때 만들어진 것으로, 무려 90년이나 지난 매우 낡은 지도였다.'

- 2004년 7월 19 AFP통신 -

90년이나 지난 낡은 지도로 여행한 할아버지의 신문 기사 내용을 읽으며 실컷 웃은 적이 있다. 그러다 잠시 이런 생각이 들었다. 영어 선생님인 나는 과연 어떤 지도를 들고 아이들을 가르치고 있을까? 내가 사용하고 있는 영어교수법 역시 할아버지의 낡은 지도처럼 너무나 오래된 것이어서 소용이 없는 것은 아닐까? 이런 생각을 한번쯤 해본 선생님들을 위해 최근의 교수법을 정리해 보았다. 각각의 교수법을 정독하면서 지금 자신이 서 있는 곳이 어디인지 가늠해 보기 바란다.

Part I 21세기 영어교육의 방향

1 미국 교육계의 동향

한국 영어교육에 큰 영향을 주는 나라인 미국의 교육이 어떤 방향으로 흘러가고 있는지 그 흐름을 파악하여 보자.

미국 워싱턴에 파견 근무를 나온 지 1년 반이 조금 지난 A씨는 최근 초등학교 2학년 2학기를 마친 큰 딸이 방학과 함께 들고 온 성적표를 보고 잠시 의아했다. 버지니아주 페어팩스의 한 초등학교에 다니고 있는 딸아이가 들고 온 성적표가 1개가 아니라 2개였기 때문이다. 하나는 학생의 전반적인 학업 수행을 평가한 성적표로 한국의 여느 성적표와 크게 다르지 않다. 그런데 한국에서는 볼 수 없는 또 하나의 성적표가 있었는데, 그것은 학생의 '읽기' 역량에 대한 평가였다. 어학시간에 주기적으로 주어지는 읽기 평가와 학생 스스로 독서량과 독서역량을 수시로 평가해 종합한 것이다. 미국에서는 학생들의 독서과정을 추적한 읽기평가를 아예 별도의 성적표를 통해 따로 하고 있다. 중 · 고등학교에서도 읽기, 쓰기 등을 강조하며 학생들의 독서를 특별 관리하기는 마찬가지다. 학교마다 독서전문가(reading specialist)를 두고 학생들의 어학능력을 배가시키고 있다.

미국이 이처럼 읽기, 쓰기 교육에 치중하고 있는 것과 관련해 리스 초등학교 선생님인 데이비드 씨는 "다민족 국가인 미국을 하나로 통합해 주는 게 언어의 바른 사용이기 때문일 것"이라며 "그러기 위해선 읽기, 쓰기와 자발적인 독서를 중시하는 교육이 중요하다"고 말했다.

2005년 10월 21일 매일경제

최근 통계에 따르면 미국학생 중 50% 정도가 자기 수준의 책을 독해할 수 있고, 5% 정도의 학생만이 자기 학년 수준의 글을 쓸 수 있다는 발표가 있었다. 이런 통계 발표는 매우 심각한 사회 문제로 받아들여졌고, 이 문제를 해결하기 위해 미국은 대통령까지 직접 나서기도 했다. 그 예로, 부시 대통령은 'No Child Left Behind Act (교육 수준 상향 조정법, 2001)' 을 발표했는데, 이 법을 한 마디로 요약하면 모든 학생의 읽기(reading), 쓰기(writing) 실력을 자기 학년 수준으로 올리는데 미국 역량을 집중하겠다는 것이다.

2 읽기, 쓰기를 강조하는 이유

왜 이렇게 읽기, 쓰기 교육을 강조하는 것일까? 그 이유는 미국 원어민의 경우 듣기와 말하기는 어느 정도 선천적으로 배울 수 있지만, 읽기와 쓰기는 따로 배우지 않으면 저절로 습득될 수 없기 때문이다. 특히 읽기의 경우는 학습에 있어 매우 중요한 기술로, 크게 두 부분으로 나눌 수 있는데 아래의 제시된 도표를 살펴보자.

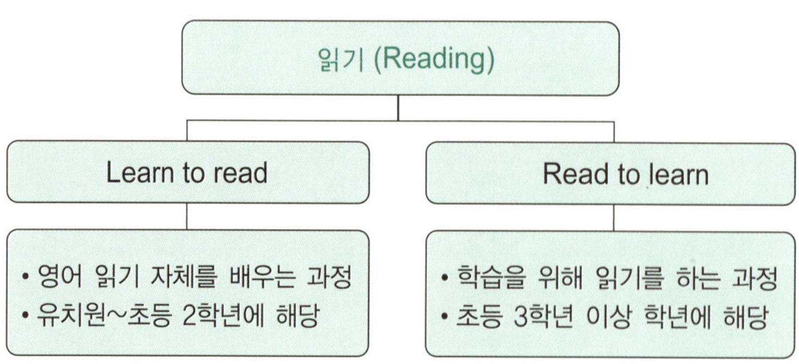

런투리드(learn to read)는 말 그 대로 영어 읽기 자체를 배우는 과정으로 유치원에서 초등 2학년 정도까지 학습하게 되며, 이 시기에는 알파벳 익히기부터 시작해서 단어와 문장 읽기를 배우게 된다. 반면 리드투런(read to learn)은 초등 3학년 이상의 학년에 적용되는 것으로 학습을 위해 읽기를 하는 것이다. 예를 들어 과학이나 사회 등의 과목을 공부하려면 해당 교과서를 읽고 이해해야 하는데, 이 때의 읽기를 리드투런(read to learn), 즉 배우기 위한 읽기라고 한다. 영어를 가르치는 교사는 자신이 가르치는 학생이 런투리드(learn to read) 과정에 있는지 아니면 리드투런(read to learn)에 있는지 늘 관심을 갖고 체크해야 한다. 경우에 따라서는 리드투런(read to learn)을 하고 있어야 할 학생이 런투리드(learn to read)조차 되지 않을 수도 있기 때문이다.

이러한 읽기 지도 접근법은 크게 두 가지로 구분된다. 부분적인 것을 먼저 학습 한 후에 전체적인 것을 이해하게 된다는 상향식 접근법(Bottom-up Approach)과 전체적인 내용을 이해하면서 세부 적인 언어 요소를 학습하는 하향식 접근법(Top-down Approach)이다. 파닉스 접근법(Phonics Approach)은 대표적인 상향식 교수법으로 우선적으로 글자를 익힌 후에 단어, 문장 순으로 학습을 하면서 작은 부분에서 큰 부분으로 확장이 되는 반면에, 총체적 언어 접근법은 대표적인 하향식 교수법으로 이야기를 먼저 배우고, 그 속에 든 문장과 단어 그리고 글자를 배우게 된다.

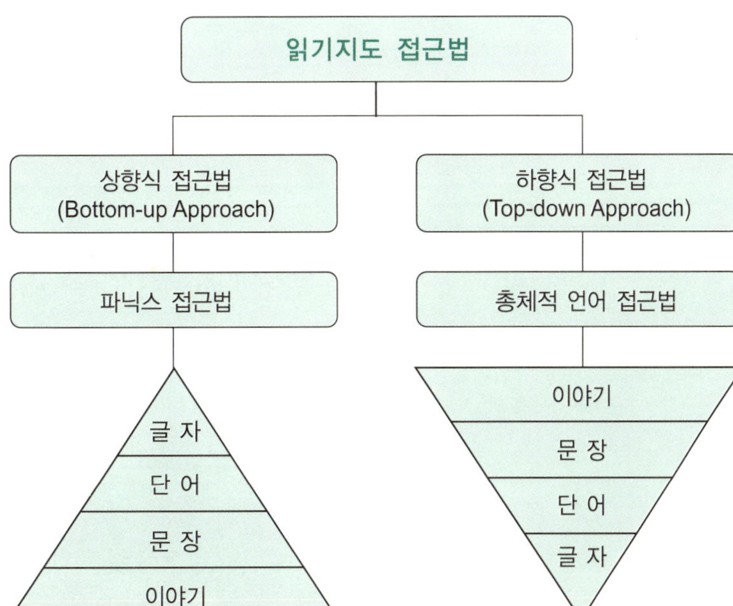

미국 교수법의 양대 산맥이라 할 수 있는 파닉스 접근법(Phonics Approach)과 총체적 언어 접근법(Whole Language Approach)은 마치 전쟁(war)에 비유될 정도로 매우 격렬하게 대립했다. 그러다가 1980년대부터 이 두 교수법의 장점을 통합해서 가르치자는 균형잡힌 교수법(Balanced Literacy Approach)이 각광받기 시작했고 앞으로도 그 인기는 지속될 것으로 보인다.

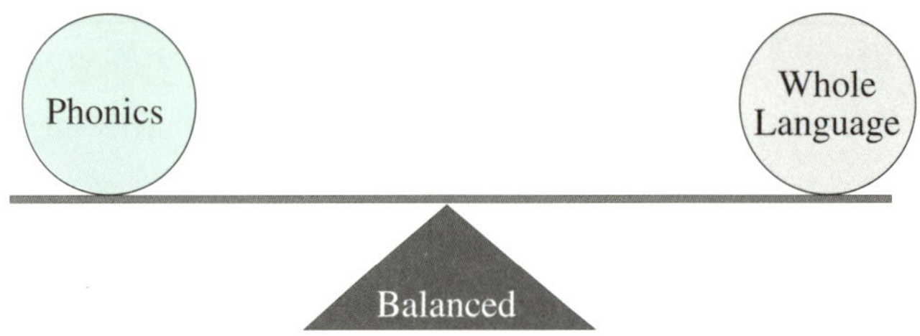

그럼, 파닉스 접근법(Phonics Approach), 총체적 접근법(Whole Language Approach), 균형잡힌 접근법(Balanced Literacy Approach)에 대해 보다 상세하게 알아보자.

3 파닉스 접근법(Phonics Approach)

1) 파닉스(Phonics)의 정의

미국 교육의 역사는 '읽기(reading)' 의 역사라 해도 과언이 아닐 정도로 모든 교수법들이 어떻게 하면 읽기를 잘할 수 있는지에 그 초점이 맞추어졌다고 볼 수 있다. 그런 방편으로 태어난 교수법 중의 하나가 바로 파닉스(Phonics)로, 파닉스란 영어를 모국어로 사용하는 아이들이 처음 문자를 접했을 때 어떤 철자에서 어떤 소리가 나오는지를 알려주는 교수법이다. 이 교수법은 1700년에서 1800년의 미국 학교에서 학습의 주류를 이루었다.

▣ 파닉스 ▣

읽기를 가르치는 방법으로, 철자와 발음의 규칙체계를 학습하는 것이다.

(A method of teaching reading by studying the relationship between thc lcttcr and the sound.)

– Halvorson 1992 –

이러한 파닉스 학습은 소리를 강조하는 학습으로, 단어를 분해해서 읽는 기술에 그 초점이 맞춰졌다. 예를 들어 학생이 'cat' 이라는 새로운 단어를 배우게 될 경우, 교사는 'cat' 이라는 단어의 개별 소리를 분리(sound out)해서 말해 주게 된다.

T : Today' s new word is 'cat'.

(오늘 배울 새로운 단어는 'cat' 입니다.)

'Cat' would be sounded out as "c–a–t".

('cat' 이란 단어는 c–a–t로 소리를 낼 수 있어요.)

이처럼 파닉스란 알파벳 26자가 가지고 있는 소리와의 규칙을 습득하여 정확하게 읽기와 쓰기를 할 수 있도록 고안된 교수법이다.

2) 파닉스(Phonics) 용어 정리

파닉스와 관련된 용어를 정리해 보자. 다른 책에서는 '이중 모음' 이나 '혼성음' 처럼 파닉스 용어를 우리말로 번역해 놓은 경우가 많은데, 이것이 오히려 개념을 이해하는데 방해가 될 수도 있기 때문에 모음(vowels)과 자음(consonants)을 제외한 다른 용어들은 영어로만 표기해 놓았다.

Vowels(모음)	자음이 아닌 철자 'a, e, i, o, u' 와 단어의 끝에 오는 y 가 모음이다. 예 ant, egg, insect, ox, union, baby
Consonants(자음)	철자 'a, e, i, o, u' 를 제외한 철자를 자음으로 분류한다.
Consonant Blends	두 개 혹은 두 개 이상의 자음이 겹쳐서 각각의 소리 그대로 발음되는 것을 말한다. 예 l-blends(bl, cl, fl, gl, pl, sl) r-blends(br, cr, dr, fr, gr, pr, tr) s-blends(sc, sk, sm, sn, sp, st, sw, scr, squ, str, spr, spl) 기타 : tw, thr, qu
Consonant Digraphs	두 개의 자음이 겹쳐서 전혀 새로운 소리를 내는 것을 말한다. 예 sh, th, th, ch, gh, ph, wh,
Vowel Blends (Diphthongs)	모음 두 개가 연달아 나오는데, 이 두 모음의 관계가 매우 밀착되어 있어서 이 두 모음을 하나의 발음 단위로 취급하는 경우를 말한다. 즉, 모음의 개수는 두 개 이지만 소리는 하나로 취급한다. 예 oi(foil), oy(toy), ou(bound), ow(cow)
Vowel Digraphs	두 개의 모음이 연달아 나오는데, 두 개의 모음이 합쳐져서 하나의 새로운 소리를 나는 경우를 말한다. 예 au(caught), aw(saw), oo(food)

3) 교실에서 활용할 수 있는 파닉스(Phonics) 자료

다음은 알파벳과 알파벳의 대표 소리를 정리한 도표로 차트를 보면서 알파벳의 이름과, 소리, 대표 단어를 연습한다.

▣ 알파벳 차트(Alphabet Chart)

a		apple	n		nose
b		boy	o		orange
c		cat	p		pig
d		dog	q(u)		question
e		egg	r		rabbit
f		fish	s		sun
g		goat	t		tiger
h		horse	u		umbrella
i		igloo	v		violin
j		jam	w		watch
k	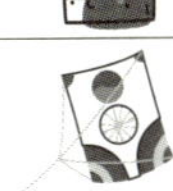	kite	x		fox
l		lamp	y		yacht
m		monkey	z		zebra

※ 참고 : 'q'의 경우 항상 'u'를 동반한다. 'x'는 끝소리가 대표소리이다.

자음 c와 g의 경우는 크게 경음(hard sound)과 연음(soft sound)으로 나눌 수 있다. hard sound로 소리나는 경우는 모음 'a, o, u'를 만날 때이고, soft sound로 소리나는 경우는 'e, i, y'를 만날 때다.

▣ 경음/연음 'c' (Hard/Soft sound 'c')

자음 c의 hard sound는 /k/이다. 해당되는 단어는 'cat, cotton, cut' 등으로 hard sound로 시작되는 단어가 많기 때문에 hard sound부터 가르친다.

soft sound의 발음은 /s/로 해당되는 단어는 'center, city, cyber' 등이다.

a o u	c	e i y
cat		cell
cotton		city
cut		cyber
Hard sound		Soft sound

▣ 경음/연음 'g' (Hard/Soft sound 'g')

자음 g의 hard sound는 /g/이다. 해당되는 단어는 'gate, go, gut' 등으로 hard sound로 시작되는 단어가 많기 때문에 hard sound부터 가르친다.

soft sound의 발음은 /dʒ/로 해당되는 단어는 'gentle, giant, gym' 등이다.

a o u	g	e i y
gate		gentle
go		giant
gut		gym
Hard sound		Soft sound

파닉스 수업 시간에는 'subway'의 'sub–'처럼 단어 앞에 붙는 접두사(prefixes)와 'ants'의 '–s'처럼 단어 끝에 붙는 접미사(suffixes), 'eight와 'ate'처럼 소리는 같지만 뜻은 다른 동음이의어(homophones)도 학생들에게 가르쳐야 한다. 다음은 각각의 목록을 정리한 것이다.

접두사(Prefixes)		
prefix	meaning	words
1. un	not, opposite of	unfriendly
2. re	again	replace,
3. in, im, ir, ill	not	impossible
4. dis	not, opposite of	dishonest
5. en	in	encourage
6. non	not	nonsense
7. in, im	in or into	include
8. over	too much	overpower
9. mis	wrongly	mistake
10. sub	under	subway
11. pre	before	preschool
12. inter	between, among	interchange
13. fore	before	forehead
14. de	opposite of	devalue
15. trans	across	transportation
16. super	above	superman
17. semi	half	semifinal
18. anti	against	antifreeze
19. mid	middle	midterm
20. under	below	underground

접미사(Suffixes)		
suffix	meaning	words
1. s, es	plurals	ants, foxes
2. ed	past-tense verbs	walked
3. ing	present participle	singing
4. ly	adverb form	slowly
5. er, or	person connected	farmer, doctor
6. ion, tion	act, process	solution
7. ible, able	can be done	capable
8. al, ial	characteristic of	ideal
9. y	characterized by	discovery
10. ness	state of	happiness
11. ity, ty	state of	possibility
12. ment	action	punishment
13. ic	characteristic of	specific
14. ous, eous, ious	have the qualities of	humorous
15. en	made of	wooden
16. er	comparative	bigger
17. ive, ative	adjective form	talkative
18. ful	full of	beautiful
19. less	without	careless
20. est	comparative	biggest

제시한 접두사, 접미사 목록은 「*Word Frequency Book*(Carroll, Davies, and Richman, 1971)」에서 발췌한 것으로 가장 빈번하게 사용되는 순서대로 나열한 것이다.

동음이의어(Homophones)		
aloud/allowed	made/maid	so/sew
ate/eight	mail/male	some/sum
bear/bare	main/mane	son/sun
beat/beet	meet/meat	stare/stair
blew/blue	night/knight	steal/steel
brake/break	not/knot	tale/tail
by/buy	oh/owe	there/their/they're
cent/sent	one/won	through/threw
deer/dear	peace/piece	tied/tide
do/due/dew	peak/peek	toe/tow
fare/fair	pear/pair	two/to/too
flour/flower	plain/plane	waist/waste
for/four	read/reed	way/weigh
hair/hare	real/reel	weak/week
heal/heel	right/write	wear/where
heard/herd	road/rode	weight/wait
here/hear	roll/role	whole/hole
horse/hoarse	rose/rows	wood/would
hour/our	sail/sale	wrap/rap
I/eye	see/sea	
knew/new	seem/seam	
know/no	seen/scene	
knows/nose		

제시한 동음이의어는 소리는 같지만 철자가 다른 단어를 정리한 것으로, 미국의 경우 초등학교 1학년 학기 초에 아이들에게 가르친다. 활용법으로는 두 개의 문장을 제시한 후, 각 문장에 알맞은 단어를 적어 넣게 한다.

예 flour / flower

- Bread is made from ( ).: 빵은 ( )으로 만든다.
- Roses are my favorite ( ).: 장미는 내가 가장 좋아하는 ( )이다.

4) 영어사전 사이트

다음은 인터넷에서 활용 가능한 영어사전 사이트를 정리해 놓은 것이다.

http://www.enchantedlearning.com/Dictionary.html로 가서 상단에 보이는 알파벳을 클릭하면 단어의 의미와 그림까지 얻을 수 있는 사이트이다.

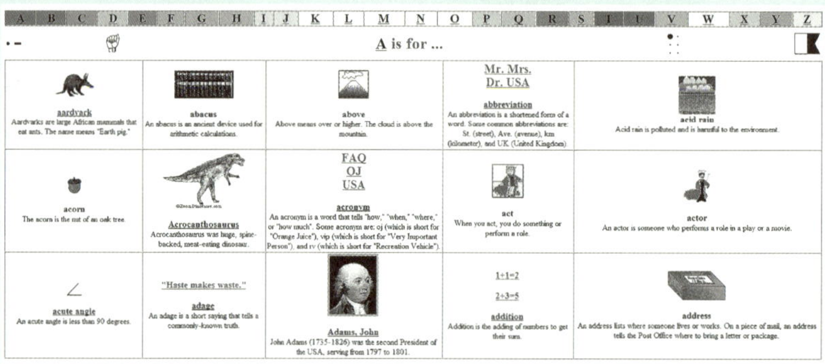

http://www.et05.com →영단어영역→왼쪽 하단 메뉴 바의 **그림영어사전** 클릭 그림과 예시문장이 나와 있고, 발음도 들을 수 있다.

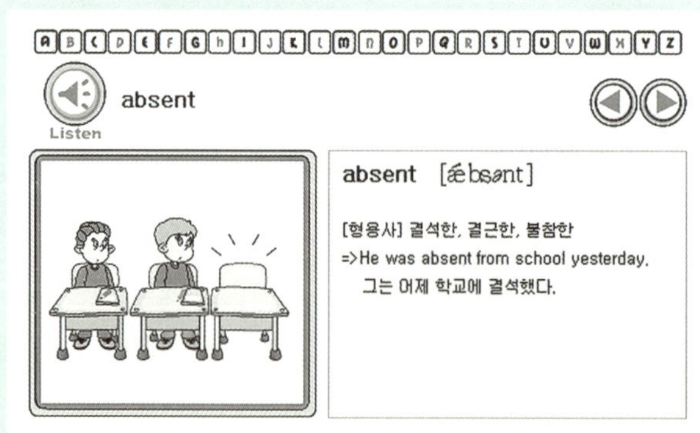

http://www.pidic.com/ : 단어의 그림을 볼 수 있고, 상세한 단어 설명이 도움이 된다.

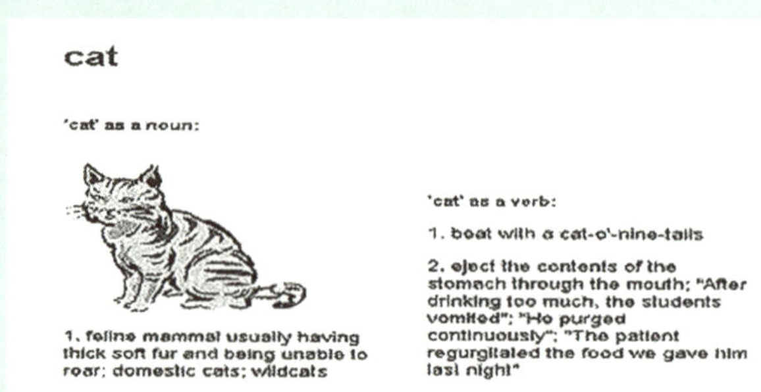

시중에 나와 있는 파닉스 교재 중에서 좋은 교재를 고를 수 있는 기준은 앞서 말한 파닉스 내용을 충실히 담고 있는 것을 선택하는 것이다. 특히 영어를 처음 시작한 아이들의 경우에는 시각적 자료, 즉 그림이 풍부한 교재를 선택해야 한다. 아이들은 그림의 이미지를 통해 언어를 간접 경험하게 되기 때문이다.

5) 파닉스(Phonics) 학습의 한계

읽기는 영어의 뿌리 단계라고 할 수 있다. 그 뿌리가 얼마나 튼튼한가에 따라 영어라는 열매의 크기가 좌우된다. 여기서 우리가 기억해야 할 것은 영어를 잘 읽는다는 것의 정의이다. 영어를 잘 읽는다는 것은 소리 내서 단어를 읽어 내는 수준을 말하는 것이 아니다. 그 궁극적인 목표는 '내용 이해(comprehension)', 즉 영어를 읽어 내면서 그 의미를 이해할 수 있는 수준이 목표이다. 이 목표에 도달하기 위한 방법 중의 하나가 파닉스 학습으로, 이러한 파닉스 학습은 장점과 단점을 동시에 가지고 있다.

▣ Phonics 학습의 장점 ▣

1. 알파벳의 각 letter에는 이름과 소리가 있다는 것을 익혀줌으로써 단어의 발음을 쉽게 할 수 있다.
2. 발음기호를 찾기 위해 사전을 찾을 필요가 없다.
3. 철자를 무조건 무의미하게 암기하는 대신 소리를 통해 철자를 학습하기 때문에 철자를 쉽게 기억할 수 있다.
4. 학생들이 사전이나 교사를 의존하지 않고 단어나 문장을 스스로 읽음으로써 만족감과 자신감을 얻을 수 있다.

▣ Phonics 학습의 단점 ▣

1. 논리력이 부족한 어린 아이에게는 적합하지 않은 교수법이다.
2. 말하기가 서투른 초기 학습자에게는 효과가 떨어진다.
3. 모든 규칙이 100% 적용되는 것이 아니다.
4. 읽기의 일부분일 뿐 읽기의 완성이 아니다.

파닉스 학습에서는 연습문제(worksheets)를 풀어 보는데 많은 시간을 할애하고 있고, 상당수의 학생들이 이런 단순 반복학습 활동을 힘들어한다. 그런데 이러한 파닉스 위주의 교육이 집중적으로 진행된 후인 1970년도에 이루어진 연구 조사의 결과, 놀랍게도 미국인의 33%가 책을 읽지 못하는 것으로 드러났다. 이에 반기를 들고 일어난 교수법이 총체적 언어적 접근(Whole Language Approach)이다.

4 총체적 언어 접근법(Whole Language Approach)

Whole Language Approach는 원래 모국어를 읽고 쓸 줄 모르는 미국과 캐나다 문맹자들을 대상으로 개발되어 1980년대 중반 경부터 각광을 받아온 교수법으로, 종래의 획일화된 언어교육에 반대하여 일어났다. Whole Language Approach에 영향을 준 주요 이론가로는 아동중심 교육의 John Dewey, 언어학습과 사고에 관련하여 Jean Piaget 와 Vygotsky, 그리고 언어교육의 이론적 기반을 제공한 Holdaway를 꼽을 수 있다. 이들의 주장을 종합해 보면, 모든 언어와 경험이 교수 목적으로 사용될 수 있고, 또 그렇게 될 때 학습자는 흥미를 느끼고 학습활동에 능동적으로 참여하게 되어 진정한 언어 학습이 이루어지게 된다는 것으로, 처음부터 언어를 상황 속에서 가르치는데 듣기, 말하기, 읽기, 쓰기를 따로 분리하여 가르치지 않고 의사소통 상황 속에서 저절로 익혀지도록 하는 방법인 것이다. 이러한 Whole Language Approach에 대해 보다 구체적으로 알아보자.

1) 총체적 언어 접근법(Whole Language Approach)의 개념

총체적 언어 접근법은 하나의 교수법이라기보다는 인간의 가치를 존중하는 철학이라고 말할 수 있다. 전통적인 학습 방법은 학문에 중점을 두고, 그것을 아느냐 모르느냐를 따지는 것이라면, 총체적 언어 접근법은 인본주의에 바탕을 두고 있기 때문에 결과보다는 과정을 중시하고, 전통적인 교육방법에서 실시되는 낙제와 같은 제도는 두지 않는다. 또한 학생들은 자기 힘으로 학습하는 법을 알고 있다는 사실에서 출발하기 때문에 교사는 학생을 가르치는 사람이라기보다는 학생을 도와 주는 사람이라고 여긴다. 또한 기존의 전통적 언어교육에서는 언어를 듣기, 말하기, 읽기, 쓰기의 네 가지 영역으로 분리하여 가르쳤지만, 총체적 언어 접근법에서는 이 네 가지 기능을 분리하지 않고 통합하여 가르친다.

2) 총체적 언어 접근법(Whole Language Approach)의 특징 및 학습활동

학자 G. S. Anderson은 총체적 언어교수법의 특징을 다음의 세 가지로 말하고 있다.

총체적 언어 교수법을 통한 언어학습은 첫째, 의미 있고 자연스러운 언어여야 하고, 둘째, 단편적인 조각이 아닌 총체적인 언어이어야 하며, 셋째, 의미 있는 텍스트를 통해 학습이 이루어져야 한다고 말하고 있다. 총체적 언어교육은 무엇보다도 학습자의 입장에서 그들에게 진정으로 의미 있는 언어학습이 되게 하는데 초점을 둔다.

따라서, 총체적 언어 접근법에 의해 수업이 이뤄지는 교실 현장에서는 철저하게 학생 중심의 활동이 주가 된다. 특히 언어수업 시간의 경우에는 생생한 자료를 활용하며, 교실 밖에서 실제 사용되고 있는 언어를 사용하여 수업을 진행한다. 이러한 학습활동을 정리해 보면 다음과 같다.

① 학습은 전체로부터 부분으로, 구체적인 것에서부터 추상적인 것으로, 친숙한 것으로부터 친숙하지 않은 것으로 진행된다. 따라서 개인별, 소집단 별 읽기와 쓰기, 일기 쓰기, 포트폴리오 쓰기, 토의 작문, 학습자가 만든 책, 이야기 쓰기 등의 활동들이 대부분이다.

② 총체적 언어 접근법에서는 특정한 교재를 사용하지 않고, 활동도 미리 정해진 것이 없으며, 학습자의 관심과 학생 자신의 학습 목표에 적합한 과업을 수행한다.

③ 학교에서의 학습은 마치 집에서 이뤄지는 것처럼 편안하게 이뤄지고, 기존의 전통적 교실에서는 제일 우수한 학생의 작품만을 전시해 놓는데 반해, 총체적 언어 접근법을 적용한 교실은 학생과 교사의 작품으로 가득 채운다.

④ 수업을 진행할 때도 경쟁보다는 협동을 중시한다.

3) 총체적 언어 접근법(Whole Language Approach)에서의 교사의 역할

그렇다면 기존의 전통적 교수법에서의 교사의 역할과 총체적 언어 접근법에서의 교사의 역할이 어떻게 다른지 정리해 보자.

① 전통적 교사는 모든 것을 직접 가르치지만, 총체적 언어 접근법에서는 학생들의 학

습을 촉진하는 역할을 한다.

② 교사는 학생들을 성적으로 분류하지 않는다.

③ 교사는 학생들에게 학습의 선택권을 주어서, 학생들이 좋아하는 텍스트를 고르게 한다.

④ 교사는 학생들에게 위험을 무릅쓰고, 모험할 수 있는 용기를 북돋우게 한다.

⑤ 교사들이 먼저 가르치지 않고, 아이들의 머릿속에서 있는 기본 지식에서 학습을 시작한다.

⑥ 추상적인 것은 가급적 피하고, 반드시 예를 들어 설명한다.

⑦ 전통적 교사는 학생들에게만 읽기와 쓰기를 시키지만, 총체적 언어 접근법에서는 교사가 학생의 모델 역할을 해야 하기 때문에, 교사가 학생과 함께 직접 읽고, 쓰기를 같이 한다.

4) 총체적 언어 접근법(Whole Language Approach)에서의 교실활동

지금껏 총체적 언어 접근법의 개념과 특징, 교사의 역할을 알아봤다. 그렇다면 실제 교실에서는 어떤 수업이 이뤄지는지 구체적인 활동을 알아보자.

총체적 언어 접근법에서 중요하게 여겨지는 것은 바로 의미 있는 책읽기 활동이다. 따라서 실제 교실에서 사용되는 교재는 작가들이 쓴 문학작품을 주로 사용한다. 이러한 문학작품으로 수업을 할 때는 교사는 큰 소리로 작품을 읽어 준다. 그 다음에는 단어를 가리키면서 읽어 준다. 이런 모델 역할을 하는 교사를 보면서, 학생들은 어떻게 읽기를 해야 하는지 그 방법을 배우게 된다. 그런 후에 학생들과 교사는 함께 책을 읽고, 최후에는 학생 스스로 혼자서 책을 읽는 과정에 도달하게 한다. 이런 읽기 활동을 한 후에는 학생 스스로 포트폴리오를 만드는 작업으로 활동을 마무리한다. 포트폴리오의 구체적인 예로는 미니북을 만들거나, 혹은 직접 연극을 해봄으로써 영어가 의미 있는 언어로 받아들여지게 된다.

5) 총체적 언어 접근법(Whole Language Approach)의 한계

총체적 언어교수법은 많은 장점을 가진 교수법이다. 그러나 그런 장점에도 불구하고 다수를 대상으로 하는 교육에서는 이상적인 교수법에 불과하다는 비판을 받게 된다. 특히나 총체적 언어교수법으로 지도를 받은 학생들의 읽기, 쓰기 능력이 기존의 전통적 교수법으로 교육받은 경우보다 더 떨어지게 되자, 총체적 언어교수법은 이상적이긴 하지만 비효율적이라는 지적을 받게 되었다. 휴머니즘의 철학, 과정을 중시, 낙제 철폐 등 의도는 모두 좋았으나, 그 결과 미국 아이들의 문맹률이 더욱 높아졌기 때문이다. 예를 들어 미 연방정부는 삼천억 달러가 넘는 거액의 돈을 타이틀 원(Title I)이란 이름아래 환경이 안 좋은 아이들의 교육에 투자해 왔지만, 40년이 지난 후, 미국 전역의 공립학교 4학년 중에서 겨우 32 퍼센트만이 제대로 읽을 수 있는 수준이라는 참담한 결과가 나왔다. Whole Language Approach에 의해 학생을 가르치고 나니 파닉스 위주의 수업을 할 때보다 아이들의 읽기 수준이 더 떨어졌다는 것이다. 급기야 이런 문제는 국가적인 차원에서 그 중요성을 강조하기 시작하였고, 그 예로, 1997년에는 모든 아이들이 초등 3학년 말까지 읽기를 배워야 한다는 미 연방정부의 'Reading Excellence Act' 조항이 발표되기도 했다.

> "We must do more…… to make sure every child can read well by the end of the third grade."
>
> (3학년 말까지는 모든 아이들이 읽기를 할 수 있게 모든 조치를 취해야 합니다.)
>
> -1997년 빌 클린턴 대통령의 국회 연설 중에서

그러나 그 후에도 미국 아이들의 읽기 실력은 나아지질 않았고, 아이들의 낮은 읽기 수준에 충격을 받은 미 정부는 'No Child Left Behind Act'란 법령을 발표하였다. 발표내용의 요지는 아이들에게 읽는 것을 가르치는 것이 가장 중요한 일이고, 아이들의 수준에 따라 읽는 기준을 마련하고, 시험을 강화해서 문맹률을 낮춰보자는 것이다.

"We have an obligation to meet the goal to make sure every child can read at grade level."
(모든 아이들이 각 학년 수준의 글을 읽을 수 있게끔 하는 것이 우리의 의무 입니다.)
- 2001년 부시 대통령의 연설문 중에서

이처럼, 미국 교육의 역사에서 핵심 과제는 바로 'Reading' 이었다. 이런 과제를 해결하고자 미국의 교육학자들은 파닉스 학습과 총체적 언어 교육을 절충하여 내놓은 것이 바로 균형잡힌 접근법(Balanced Literacy Approach)이다.

5 균형잡힌 접근법(Balanced Literacy Approach)

1) 균형잡힌 접근법(Balanced Literacy Approach)의 개념

1980년대에 확산되기 시작했으며, 향후에도 그 영향력은 더욱 커지고 있는 Balanced Literacy Approach의 뜻은 말 그대로 '균형을 이룬' 접근법이다. 즉 파닉스나 총체적 언어 접근법 그 어느 한쪽에도 치우치지 않고, 두 가지 교수법의 장점을 최대한 수용하고, 접목시켰다는 데 그 의미가 있다. 이러한 Balanced Literacy Approach의 정의는 다음과 같다.

▣ 균형잡힌 교수법(Balanced Literacy Approach) ▣

교사가 매일 매일 심사숙고하여, 학생 모두가 보다 나은 독자(reader)와 작가(writer)가 될 수 있도록 최선의 학습 방법을 결정하는 교수법

(A decision-making approach through which a teacher makes thoughtful decisions each day about the best way to help each child become a better reader and writer.)

이러한 균형잡힌 교수법은 동화책 등의 의미 있는 교재를 통해서 아이들에게 내용 이해라는 언어의 큰 틀을 먼저 맛보게 한 후 그 안에서 나온 단어를 중심으로 phonics 의 요소를 접목시켜 읽기를 가르치는 것이 이 접근법의 핵심이라 할 수 있다.

2) 균형잡힌 프로그램(Balanced Literacy Program)

Balanced Literacy Approach에 있는 'Literacy'의 사전적 의미를 살펴보면, 'the ability to read and write', 즉 '읽고 쓰는 능력'이라고 되어 있다. 즉 Balanced Literacy Approach의 중점과제는 'reading' 과 'writing'인 것이다. 이 Balanced Literacy Program을 도표로 나타내면 다음과 같다.

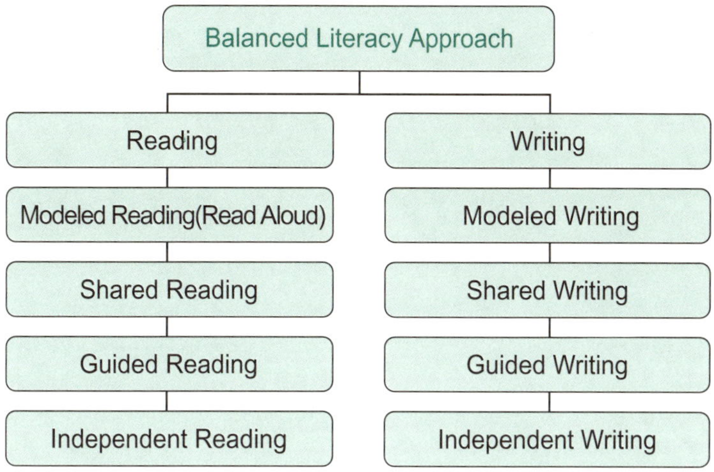

도표에서 알 수 있듯이 Balanced Literacy Approach란 읽기와 쓰기를 두 축으로 해서 제시된 단계를 거쳐 최종적으로 혼자서 읽고, 혼자서 쓸 수 있는 단계까지 이끌어 주는 교수법을 말한다. 다음은 각 단계의 내용을 간략하게 정리한 것이다.

Reading Program	
Modeled Reading(Read Aloud): *"I Do It, You Watch"* Teacher reads aloud selections to students (교사가 선택한 글을 학생들에게 큰 소리로 읽어주는 것)	**Shared Reading:** *"I Do It, You Help"* Teacher and students read text together (교사와 학생이 텍스트를 함께 읽는 것)
Guided Reading: *"You Do It, I Help"* Teacher works with a group of students similar in strengths and needs and provides instruction through mini-lessons (수준이 비슷한 학생들이 모인 그룹과 함께 미니수업을 통해서 지도를 받으며 읽기를 하는 것)	**Independent Reading:** *"You Do It, I Watch"* Students read independently (학생 스스로 읽기를 하는 것)

Writing Program	
Modeled Writing: *"I Do It, You Watch"* Modeled writing is the teacher being an active writer. (교사가 학생들 앞에서 글을 쓰는 모습을 시범적으로 보여주는 것)	**Shared Writing:** *"I Do It, You Help"* Teacher and students collaborate to write text. (교사와 학생이 공동으로 글을 쓰는 것)
Guided Writing: *"You Do It, I Help"* Teacher works with a group of students similar in strengths and needs and provides instruction through mini-lessons(교사와 비슷한 수준의 학생들이 모여 함께 미니수업을 통해서 지도를 받으며 쓰기를 하는 것)	**Independent Writing:** *"You Do It, I Watch"* Students write independently (학생 스스로 쓰기를 하는 것)

6 학년별 읽기 자료

그렇다면 각 학년별로 읽어야 하는 읽기의 수준은 어느 정도일까? 다음에 제시되는 학년별 글을 읽고 문제를 풀어 보자.(이 자료는 http://www.pearsonlongman.com에서 발췌한 것이다.)

Grade 1

How They Grow by Judy Nayer

How does a butterfly grow? It starts out as a tiny egg. It becomes a caterpillar. It eats lots of leaves. It grows and grows. Then it goes inside a cocoon. At last, it comes out. It' s a butterfly!

How does a frog grow? It starts out as a tiny egg in the water. The egg grows into a tadpole. It keeps changing. It eats tiny plants. It grows and grows. At last, it hops out of the pond. It's a frog!

How does a flower grow? It starts out as a seed. Sun and rain help the seed grow. Roots grow into the ground. The plant grows and grows. At last, a bud opens. It's a flower! Now you know how they grow!

Q1. What do you think the butterfly will do next?

① fly away ② turn into a frog
③ sing a song ④ swim in the water

Q2. Where does a tadpole live?

① in a tree ② under a rock
③ in the sky ④ in the water

Q3. Read this sentence from the story. At last, it hops out of the pond. What does hops mean?

① runs ② jumps
③ falls ④ swims

Grade 2

Blueberries by Wanda Hann

Do you know how blueberries grow? They grow on bushes. Each blueberry is small and round. Many blueberries can grow on one bush. At first, the blueberries are green. The green berries are not ready to eat yet. They need a lot of sun and rain to help them become fat and sweet. When the berries turn blue, they are ripe and ready to be picked.

Some farmers grow blueberries in big fields. The people who live nearby can earn money by helping to pick the blueberries. Each one takes a pail out to the field and fills it with blueberries. They work fast so that they can fill many pails. They want to earn as much money as they can. When they are done picking, their fingers are blue from the juice of the berries!

After the blueberries are picked, they are put into boxes and sent to stores. People buy the blueberries and take them home to eat. Some people like to wash the berries and eat them one by one. Other people like to cook with blueberries. They make blueberry muffins and pancakes.

No matter how you eat them, blueberries taste great!

Q1. The people who live nearby can earn money by helping to pick the blueberries. What does earn mean?

① sell ② get

③ lose ④ share

Q2. What color are the blueberries BEFORE they are ready to be picked?

① blue ② red

③ green ④ brown

Q3. Where do the blueberry pickers work?

① in a barn ② in a field

③ in a forest ④ near a stream

Q4. What happens to blueberries AFTER they are picked?

① They are put into boxes. ② They need sun and rain.

③ Farmers plant them. ④ They become sweet and ripe.

Q5. What could be another title for this story?

① "All About Blueberries" ② "How to Cook with Blueberries"

③ "Eating Blueberries" ④ "All About Strawberries"

Grade 3

Outer Space by Meish Goldfish

From far out in space, Earth looks like a blue ball. Since water covers three - fourths of the Earth' s surface, blue is the color we see most. The continents look brown, like small islands floating in the huge, blue sea. White clouds wrap around the Earth like a light blanket. The Earth is shaped like a sphere, or a ball. It is 25,000 miles around! It would take more than a year to walk around the whole planet. A spaceship can fly around the widest part of the sphere in only 90 minutes.

Even though spaceships have traveled to the Moon, people cannot visit the Moon without special suits. The Moon has no air or water. Plants and animals can' t live there either.

Astronauts first landed on the Moon in 1969. After that, there were six more trips to the Moon. They brought back Moon rocks, which scientists are still studying. There are holes, or craters, all over the Moon' s surface. Scientists believe that meteorites smashed into the Moon millions of years ago and formed the craters.

The Sun is the closest star to Earth. A star is a hot ball of burning gas. The Sun looks very big because it is so close. But the Sun is just a medium - sized star. Billions of far - away stars are much bigger than our Sun. The burning gases from the Sun are so hot that they warm the Earth from 93 million miles away! Even though the Sun is always glowing, the night here on Earth is dark. That's because the Earth rotates, or turns around, every 24 hours. During the day, the Earth faces the Sun. Then we see light. During the night, the Earth turns away from the Sun. Then it faces the darkness of space.

Each day we learn more about the Earth, the Moon, and the Sun.

Q1. Why is blue the color we see most when looking at Earth from outer space?

① Because most of the Earth is covered in land.

② Because the Sun's rays make the Earth look blue.

③ Because most of the Earth is covered in water.

④ Because clouds wrap around the Earth.

Q2. Read this sentence from the story. Scientists believe that meteorites smashed into the Moon millions of years ago and formed the craters.

What does formed mean?

① hit　　② made

③ broke　　④ stopped

Q3. What causes daylight on Earth?

① The full Moon causes daylight.

② Daylight is caused by the Earth facing away from the Sun.

③ The heat of the Sun's rays causes daylight.

④ Daylight is caused by the Earth facing toward the Sun.

Q4. Which of the following sentences BEST describes the Sun?

① The Sun looks small because it is so far from Earth.

② The Sun is a ball of burning gases that gives the Earth heat and light.

③ The Sun is a small star.

④ The Sun is not as hot as it looks.

Q5. Why did the astronauts bring rocks back from the Moon?

① Because they didn't know if they would return to the Moon ever again.

② Because they wanted to prove that they went to the Moon.

③ Because they wanted to remember how the Moon looked.

④ Because they wanted to study them and learn more about the Moon.

Q6. What is the main idea of the article?

① Plants and animals can't live on the Moon.

② Without the Sun we would have no heat or light.

③ We know a lot about the Earth, Moon, and Sun, but there is still more to learn.

④ From outer space, the Earth looks tiny, even though it is thousands of miles around.

Grade 4

How the Chipmunk Got Its Stripes
A Legend of the Lroquois

Long ago, the Earth was covered in darkness. None of the creatures living there knew what daylight looked like.

One day, all of the animals of the forest gathered together in a clearing. They wondered if it would be better to remain in darkness, or if it would be better to also have light. Deer, Chipmunk, Raccoon, Wolf, Bear, and many other creatures climbed to the top of the highest mountain. The mountain stood so tall that there were no trees on its top, and it was covered only with rocks. Millions of stars blinked in the dark sky overhead. The biggest and most powerful animal in the forest was the bear, and he was the first to reach the mountaintop. Bear stood on the highest peak, looked out over the forest below, and argued for remaining in darkness. He said that the creatures of the forest would be able to sleep better in darkness because there would be no light to keep them awake. Most of the other animals were afraid, and they agreed with Bear. Raccoon said that he did not mind the darkness because he was so smart that he could find plenty of food, even in the dark. Wolf was easy to please, too. She didn' t mind the darkness because she could howl in darkness or in light.

But one animal did stand up to Bear. Chipmunk, the smallest of the animals, argued that it would be better to have both light and dark. Chipmunk was very clever. As Bear continued to argue for darkness, she made many good arguments for light.

Slowly, the night passed. Bear grew tired of talking, but Chipmunk chattered on and on, as if she had all of the energy in the world. As the other animals dropped off to sleep, one by one, Chipmunk kept arguing.

Finally, the first sunrise ever seen by the animals appeared over the top of the mountain. They woke up and were amazed by what they saw.

Chipmunk began to dance from rock to rock. Bear became angry because he didn't get his way. He roared loudly and ran after Chipmunk. He chased Chipmunk all the way down the mountain. Bear was fast, and he reached out his giant paw to grab Chipmunk. Chipmunk got away, but not before Bear managed to scratch her back with his long claws. And that is why, to this day, you can see stripes on Chipmunk's back!

Q1. What is the theme of this story?

① Stand up for what you believe in.
② It is always better to go along with the crowd.
③ There is only one right way to do things.
④ Making decisions is easy.

Q2. What is Bear like?

① He is a good listener.
② He is used to getting his way.
③ He is unsure about what he wants.
④ He is well liked by the other animals.

Q3. Bear grew tired of talking, but Chipmunk chattered on and on, as if she had all the energy in the world.

What does chattered mean?

① moved slowly ② laughed
③ spoke quickly ④ argued

Q4. Where does the story take place?

① in a barn
② on an island
③ near a lake
④ on a mountaintop

Q5. What happened after Chipmunk's argument with Bear?

① The animals saw their first sunrise ever.

② Bear was happy that he got his way.

③ The animals continued to live in darkness.

④ Chipmunk fell asleep.

Q6. Read this sentence from the story.

Chipmunk, the smallest of animals, argued that it would be better to have both light and darkness. What is an antonym for the word argued?

① whispered ② agreed

③ jumped ④ yelled

Grade 5

It's All Clear Now by Jean Lawler

It all started at the beginning of fifth grade. At first, Carmen wasn't really sure what was happening. In class, she had to squint to see the blackboard clearly. She had to do the same thing when she read street signs, or when she watched a movie. As the fuzziness got worse, she became more and more worried. It was important for her to see the notes and homework assignments the teacher put on the board.

It wasn't long before Carmen found herself squinting all the time, but she didn't want anyone to know that she was having a problem seeing. In class, she asked for a desk that was closer to the blackboard. One day, her teacher said, "Carmen, are you all right? I've noticed you squinting a lot. Are you having trouble seeing the board?"

Carmen shook her head. "I'm fine, Mrs. Cruz," she said, but she knew she couldn't pretend much longer.

At home, she had to sit closer and closer to the television in order to see the picture. Her mother noticed her squinting as she watched her favorite shows, and she began to get suspicious.

"Tomorrow I' m calling the eye doctor to set up an appointment for you," she said firmly. Carmen protested, but her mother' s mind was made up.

Three days later, Carmen had new glasses and instructions from her doctor to wear them all the time. Carmen frowned in the car the whole way home.

"All of the kids at school will think I' m a nerd," she said. Her mother smiled and shook her head.

"You look just as beautiful with those glasses on as you do without them," she said. But Carmen didn' t believe her.

The next day, Carmen kept the glasses in her pocket as she walked into the schoolyard. She avoided her friends and stood alone, feeling miserable.

Suddenly, she heard her friend Theresa shout.

Carmen ran over to the other girls. "What' s wrong?" she asked.

"My silver ring is gone!" Theresa cried. "My sister sent it to me from California. It' s very special and I can' t lose it!"

Carmen could tell that Theresa was very upset. They all looked for the ring in the grassy area of the playground.

Carmen realized that she could search better if she could see better. She took the glasses out of her pocket and put them on. The objects and people around her came into sharp focus. She caught her breath. Everything looked so different! So clear! She looked down at the ground and a glimmer of silver caught her eye. It was the ring.

"Here it is," she shouted. "I've found it!" She handed it to Theresa, and Theresa slipped the ring back on her finger.

"Thanks Carmen," she said. "I never thought we'd find it." She paused. "Hey, I didn't know you wore glasses. They look great!"

Carmen had forgotten that she was wearing the new glasses. "Thanks," she replied shyly.

As they walked back toward the school building, two more girls from her class complimented her glasses. Carmen smiled. "Maybe wearing glasses won't be so bad after all," she thought.

Q1. BEFORE Carmen got glasses she thought having glasses
① wouldn't be so bad.
② wasn't able to see the blackboard clearly.
③ found Theresa's missing ring.
④ sat far away from the television.

Q2. Based on the end of the story, what do you think Carmen will do next?
① She won't tell her friends that she needs to wear glasses.
② She will keep her glasses in her pocket where no one can see them.
③ She will wear her glasses all the time.
④ She will wear her glasses only when she is with her family.

Q3. Read this sentence from the story. Her mother noticed her squinting as she watched her favorite shows, and she began to get suspicious.
What is an antonym for the word suspicious?
① doubtful ② guilty
③ innocent ④ trusting

Q4. Which statement BEST describes Carmen?

① She is willing to overcome her fears in order to help her friends.

② She doesn't care how well she does in school.

③ She cares more about herself than her friends.

④ She doesn't worry about what other people think of her.

Q5. Read this sentence from the story.

In class, she had to squint to see the blackboard clearly.

What does squint mean?

① to look with eyes partly closed

② to move closer

③ to try hard

④ to concentrate

Q6. The author's purpose in writing this story is to?

① explain how important it is to take care of your eyes at school.

② show that sometimes we imagine things will be worse then they are.

③ describe what it feels like to have to squint.

④ warn people not to wear valuable jewelry to school.

Grade 6

Popular Sports Around the Work by Kathy Mormile

For centuries, people have been playing kicking games with a ball. The game of soccer developed from some of these early games. The English probably gave soccer its name and its first set of rules. In European countries, soccer is called football or association football. Some people believe that the name "soccer" came from "assoc" an abbreviation for the word association. Others believe that the name came from the high socks that the players wear.

Organized soccer games began in 1863. In soccer, two teams of eleven players try to kick or head the ball into their opponents' goal. The goalie, who tries to keep the ball out of the goal, is the only player on the field who is allowed to touch the ball with his or her hands. The other players must use their feet, heads, and bodies to control the ball.

Every four years, soccer teams around the world compete for the World Cup. The World Cup competition started in 1930.

Brazil is the home of many great soccer players, including the most famous player of all, Pel?. With his fast footwork, dazzling speed, and great scoring ability, Pel? played for many years in Brazil and then later in New York. During his 22 years in soccer, he scored 1,281 goals and held every major record for the sport.

People in more than 140 countries around the world play soccer. It is the national sport of most European and Latin American countries. Soccer is definitely the world' s most popular sport!

James Naismith, a physical education teacher in Massachusetts, invented basketball in 1891. Naismith' s boss asked him to invent a game that students could play indoors during bad weather. He wanted to find a game that wasn' t as physically rough as soccer, football, or wrestling.

Naismith attached peach baskets to a railing ten feet above the floor at either end of the gym. The players used a soccer ball.

A person sat on a ladder next to each basket at either end of the gym, and threw out the balls that landed in the baskets. Naismith decided that having only five players on each team would keep the game from getting too rough.

Two years later, metal hoops with net bags replaced the peach baskets. Officials pulled a string on the nets to release the balls that went in. In 1894, Naismith added the backboard behind each net and changed to a larger ball. In 1913, people began using the bottomless nets that are used today.

During a basketball game, two teams of five players each throw the ball into two baskets at opposite ends of a court. Players bounce, or dribble, the ball to the basket or pass the ball to teammates. A team scores points by getting the ball into their team' s basket. The team with the highest score wins.

By the 1900s, basketball was the most popular indoor sport. Athletes in approximately 130 countries play the game. Basketball is especially popular in the United States, China, and Puerto Rico.

Baseball began in the United States in the early 1800s. Some people believe that Abner Double day invented the game.

Basketball is especially popular in the United States, China, and Puerto Rico.

Baseball began in the United States in the early 1800s. Some people believe that Abner Double day invented the game. Others think that baseball came from an old British sport called rounders. Baseball and rounders are very similar. However, in rounders the field players throw the ball right at the runner. If the ball hits the runner, he or she is out. In baseball, a field player just touches the ball to the base or the running player to get the player out.

Today' s baseball players use special equipment to help prevent injuries. Field players wear baseball gloves to protect their hands. The catcher wears a metal mask, a chest protector, and shin guards. Batters wear plastic helmets to protect their heads.

Every spring in the United States, people of all ages play baseball at local baseball fields. It' s no wonder that baseball is called the national pastime of the United States.

Q1. Which of the following events happened first?

① basketball was invented
② World Cup competition was invented
③ baseball began in the U.S.
④ organized soccer games began

Q2. Pele is a famous

① soccer player. ② baseball coach.
③ basketball player. ④ baseball player.

Q3. Read this sentence from the story.

With his fast footwork, dazzling speed, and great scoring ability, Pelé played for many years in Brazil, and then later in New York.

What does dazzling mean?

① amazing ② funny
③ light ④ difficult

Q4. What conclusion can you draw from this article?

① Sports are more popular in Brazil than in the U.S.

② Most sports involve kicking a ball.

③ Sports can be very dangerous.

④ Sports are popular in many different countries.

Q5. Read this sentence from the story. Field players wear baseball gloves to protect their hands. What is an antonym for the word protect?

① save ② harm

③ cover ④ fit

Q6. Which of the following is an opinion?

① The rules of soccer state that goalies are allowed to touch the ball with their hands.

② Basketball was first played with peach baskets attached to railings.

③ Because it is popular in so many countries, soccer is the sport that is the most fun to play.

④ In baseball, a player can touch the ball to the base or to the runner to get the runner out.

7 학년별 쓰기 자료

그렇다면 각 학년별로 글을 써내야 하는 수준은 어느 정도일까? 다음에 제시되는 학년별 글쓰기 자료를 참고하기 바란다.(이 자료는 http://www.eduplace.com에서 발췌한 것이다.)

Grade 1

Topic:

Think about a time when you were surprised in a fun or exciting way. Write a story for your teacher telling all about what happened.

Writing Sample #1;

One day I was at my friend's house. We were playing a game. Then her dad made us a tasty dinner. Later my mom came to get me. She had something in her hands. It was a cute puppy. I was so surprised! It had nice fur and a big nose. Mom let me hold the puppy in my arms. Then we drove home. I love my mom for that great surprise.

Writing Sample# 2;

Last summer my family rented a house at the seashore. I loved the seashore, but I missed Kim. Kim is my best friend. One sunny day, I was playing in the wet sand at the beach. I turned around and saw Kim. I was so surprised! Kim said, "My mom and I are going to stay with you for a whole week!" Every day Kim and I went to the beach. We filled our pails with white, black, and brown seashells. We had fun splashing and swimming in the salty waves. Kim and I had a great time! This was the best surprise.

Grade 2

Topic:

Think about a time when you were surprised in a fun or exciting way. Write a story for your teacher about a time that you were surprised. Tell what happened and how you felt.

Writing Sample #1;

On my sixth birthday, I was really surprised! My family took me to a big theme park. We went in our camper. First, we went to a nice restaurant. When we got to the table, there were candy and balloons for me. The food was really good, and for dessert I got to decorate my own cupcake. After lunch we went over to the rides. My brother was very tired, so my mom took him back to the camper. My dad and I stayed and rode a lot of the rides. My favorite rides were The Mad Racer and The Twirly Top. That night my parents had another surprise for me. They gave me my birthday presents. My mom and dad gave me a doll, and my grandma gave me a sweatshirt and sweat pants. That was such a great birthday with so many surprises!

Writing Sample# 2;

One boring summer day, I heard a loud knock on our front door. I ran to the kitchen and told my mom that someone was at the door. Mom quickly walked over and looked through the peephole. Aunt Mary had stopped by for a visit. Mom opened the door and invited her in. I said, "Hi, Aunt Mary," and gave her a hug. She was carrying something with a big blue blanket over it, and I wondered what it was. My mom and dad made some coffee for Aunt Mary. I went to my room and thought about what she had brought with her. Maybe it was a suitcase. Just then my mom called me, and I ran to the family room. Mom asked me what was different in the room. I looked around slowly and spotted something on the rug behind my dad' s favorite chair. I saw a large metal cage with a beautiful green bird inside! I ran to Aunt Mary and thanked her for my wonderful new pet. That day I got my greatest surprise ever. It was a tiny green parakeet!

Grade 3

Topic:

Imagine that you find a ring that makes you invisible. What happens after you find the ring? Write a story for your classmates telling how you find the ring and what happens when you become invisible.

Writing Sample #1;

One day I was walking down the hall. Then I saw a golden ring. I raced to go get it. Then I became invisible. I went to school. While I was in class, Mrs. Brune asked Martin if he saw me on the school bus. He told her no.

So I went into my house and stood right next to my grandma, and I called "Grandma!" She looked all around, but she didn' t see me. So I went into my room and played video games for thirty minutes.

Then I watched TV for a few minutes. Then I took a nap. When I woke up, I wasn' t invisible anymore.

Writing Sample# 2;

I went to the mall with my family one day, and we went to the movies. I found a sparkling red ring on my seat. I put the ring on. The ring was a little tight. I didn't say anything to my parents.

I just watched the movie. After the movie was over, my mom and dad couldn't see me, but they could hear my voice. They were worried. I was really scared. My parents said, "Are you playing a trick on us? Where are you?" "I'm invisible!" I shouted. So the next day we went to the doctor' s office, but the doctor said he didn' t know what to do.

We went home and kept thinking about what to do since I was still invisible. My dad made macaroni and cheese for dinner that night. He made it with lots of cheese. I like it that way. My dad said that maybe I would stop being invisible if I took off the ring. The problem was that I couldn't get the ring off. It was too tight. I kept pulling and twisting, but I still couldn't get the ring off.

My mom said I should wash my hands with soap because one time her ring came off by accident when she was washing her hands, and the ring almost went down the sink. So I washed my hands. It worked! I wasn't invisible anymore. We all started cheering. Then we decided to celebrate, so we went out for ice cream. After that I threw away the ring for good.

Grade 4

Topic:

Everyone has tried something new, such as a new food or a new sport.
Why should kids try something new? Write a paper for your teacher explaining why you think it is important for kids to try something new.

Writing Sample #1;

Here are my reasons for trying something new. First, you get to see awesome things that you have not seen before, like seeing an alligator in the water. The second thing is doing something different, like hiking seven miles up a mountain.
I didn't think I could do it, but I did it. Now I have told you my reasons.

Writing Sample# 2;

Trying something new is important, and I'll tell you all my reasons. I'm so happy when I can do something for the first time. I was petrified to try a back handspring, but my teacher said, "You can do it." So I tried it, and I actually did it! I was really happy, and my teacher was happy too. The next important thing about trying something new is I might see something I never saw before. For example, my family and I went to Colorado because we had never been there before. We saw snow for the first time. I jumped around in the fluffy snow and threw snowballs with my little brother.
When you try something new, you can tell your friends about how it turned out. I always tell my best friend, Anna, about the new things I try, and she tells me all of the fabulous new things she's tried. Anna does some pretty exciting new things. I think trying something new is important because you might learn to do something great, or you might see something you never saw before. Then you can tell your friends all about it. Whenever I try something new, I'm always glad I did it.

Grade 5

Topic:

Think of one activity you know how to do, such as swimming, in - line skating, or building a doghouse. Write a composition for your teacher explaining all about how to do this activity. Be sure to include step - by - step instructions so that someone else could do this activity.

Writing Sample #1;

I love scrambled eggs! Mom and Dad make them every Saturday. They use a skillet with butter in it so the eggs won't stick. First, they stir the eggs in a bowl. Then they pour them in the pan and stir until they're not runny anymore. We have toast and jam and orange juice too. That's it. That's my favorite breakfast. I wish we could have scrambled eggs seven days a week.

Writing Sample# 2;

Organizing? It isn't something you look forward to, but you have to do it! How can you straighten out that clump of wrinkled papers exploding from your desk or your backpack? A binder can help you whip that jumbled mess into shape, with everything in its place. To make your one - of - a - kind binder, you will need a few supplies. First, buy a binder (of course).
Choose one that's big enough for all your stuff. You'll also need some divider sheets with colored plastic tabs to label the different sections.

Last, a clear plastic zipper case is helpful for holding objects in your binder that won' t go in the rings, such as pencils, erasers, or paper clips. Now it's time to assemble the binder. First, you have to decide what is going to go in it. Do you want to include notes and handouts? Will you keep returned homework and tests here? Then sort all your papers into the sections you need. Spread the papers out around you in piles. Don't forget to make one pile for the wastebasket! You'll feel like you're drowning in paper, but don't get discouraged. Next, label each paper tab insert neatly. Write small enough so that the words will fit. Use a dark marker to make the words show through the colored plastic.

Then slide the inserts into the tabs and lay each divider on top of the pile it goes with. You're almost done! Finally, begin inserting these piles into the binder, starting with the sections that will be on the bottom and working your way up to the top. (Tip : You might want to try putting your sections in alphabetical order.) If you are including a zipper case, it should go last so that it's the first thing you see when you open your binder. Your new binder is like a file cabinet, only much lighter! It will help you find what you need quickly and easily.

Grade 6

Topic:

What if a truck carrying ten thousand frogs tipped over outside your school and the frogs got inside? Pretend this happens.

Write a story for your teacher telling all about what happens when the frogs get inside your school.

Be sure your story has a beginning, a middle, and an end.

Writing Sample ;

Once upon a school day, I heard a loud crash. We all ran outside to see what the noise was all about. To our surprise, we saw a big truck flipped on its side.

The driver was OK, so everyone headed back to class. All at once, the doors of the truck flew open. Ten thousand frogs jumped out. They swarmed over the grass and headed straight for the school. We had left the doors open, and the frogs hopped right in.

Everyone panicked. "AIEEE!" was all you could hear. Students were running everyplace, trying to get away from the frogs. The kids outside went onto the buses and got the drivers to close the doors while the kids closed the windows. The kids inside went into the locker rooms. The middle school is so crowded this year that we have two new portable classrooms. They look like giant trailers but are just like regular classrooms inside. They're only here until the new addition is finished. Most of the teachers went under the portables to hide.

After a while, we noticed that the frogs weren't after us at all. They were more interested in getting to the home economics wing. Suddenly, we heard glass shattering. The teacher had been right in the middle of a cooking demonstration, and the frogs had tipped over the vitamin juice she was mixing in the blender! Thick, green liquid went everywhere.

The frogs started swimming in the giant puddle and drinking it up. Ten thousand small frogs turned into ten thousand gigantic frogs before our very eyes. They were as big as racoons! Then I had a great idea. I said, "You inflated the frogs. Why can't you deflate them?" She helped me make a new juice. We put together the opposite of every ingredient she used in the first place. The mutant frogs shrunk until they were ten thousand normal - sized frogs.

The principal called animal control. They took care of those frogs. That afternoon, my mother asked how my day was. I just smiled and said it was typical. She would never believe the truth!

지금까지 미국 초등학교 각 학년별 읽기, 쓰기 샘플을 살펴봤다.

사실 한국에서 앞서 제시한 원고를 자기 학년의 아이들이 제대로 소화하기는 참으로 힘든 것이 현실이다. 하지만, 교사는 앞서 제시한 자료를 기준 삼아 아이들의 읽기, 쓰기의 목표를 잡아나가길 바란다. 우리 아이들이 언제까지나 낮은 수준의 단편적인 글만 읽고 있을 순 없는 일 아닌가? 아이들을 조금 더 높은 수준의 영어실력으로 이끌 수 있는 열정적인 교사가 되길 바란다.

이제, Balanced Literacy Approach의 두 핵심 축인 읽기 영역과 쓰기 영역에 대해 보다 구체적으로 살펴보자.

MEMO

Part Ⅱ
읽기(Reading)란 무엇인가?

1. 읽기의 5가지 요소 (5 Elements of Reading)
2. 읽기 과정(Reading Process)
3. 읽기 구성 요소(Reading Components)
   1) 소리내어 읽기(Modeled Reading 혹은 Read Aloud)
   2) 함께 읽기(Shared Reading)
   3) 유도된 읽기 (Guided Reading)
   4) 독립된 읽기 (Independent Reading)
4. 읽기에 대한 결론 및 당부의 말

21세기를 일컬어 정보의 홍수 시대라고 한다. 어느 미래 학자에 따르면 2020년도에는 73일을 주기로 지식의 총량이 2배씩 증가한다고 한다. 따라서 지금은 얼마나 많은 지식을 가졌느냐 보다는 자신에게 필요한 지식이 어디에 있는가(know-where), 어떻게 사용할 것인가(know-how)를 아는 것이 더 중요하다. 특히나 지식의 대부분은 읽기와 연결되어 있기 때문에, 제대로 된 읽기 능력을 가지는 것이 중요하다. 이번 장에서는 이러한 읽기(Reading)에 대해 자세히 알아보자.

Part Ⅱ 읽기란 무엇인가?

1 읽기의 5가지 기본 요소(5 Elements of Reading)

읽기란 인쇄된 문자나 글에서 뜻을 얻어 내는 인지 과정으로, 2000년도에 미국의 공식 연구기관인 전미읽기교육위원회(The National Reading Panel)에서는 읽기의 중심이 되는 다섯 가지 기본 요소를 발표했다. 이 다섯 가지 요소를 제대로 학습하지 못했을 경우, 읽기에 문제가 생긴다고 한다. 이 읽기의 다섯 가지 요소에 대해 보다 자세히 알아보자.(다음에 제시되는 내용은 「*Teaching the Essentials of Reading with Picture Books*」, Alyse Sweeney, Scholastic 에서 발췌한 것이다.)

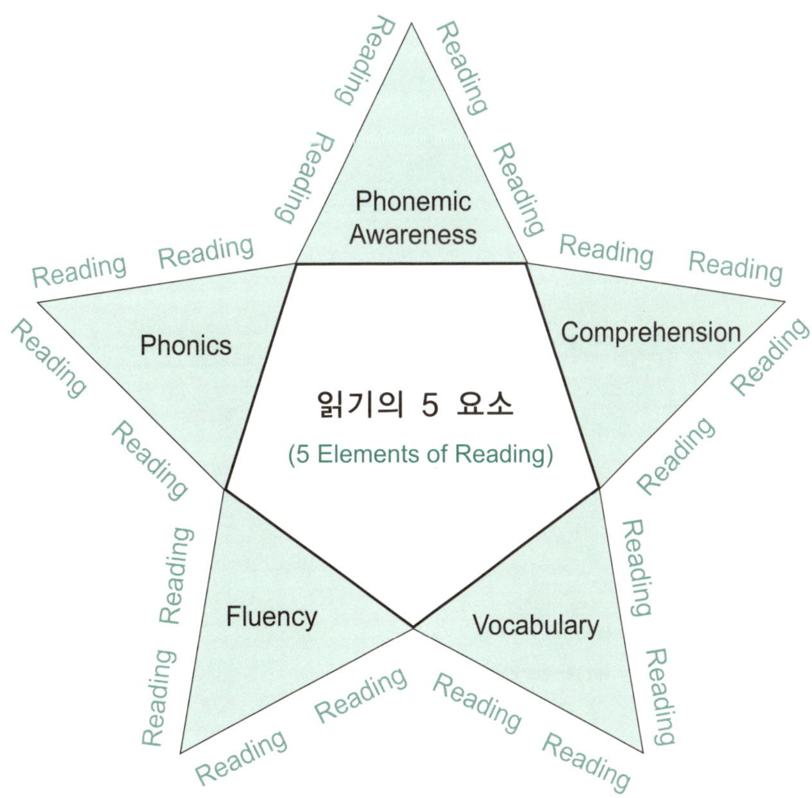

⊙ 음소인식(Phonemic Awareness)

▣ 정의

음소인식(Phonemic Awareness)이란 말을 할 때 나는 각각의 소리를 인식하고, 이 소리를 조작할 수 있는 능력을 말한다.(Phonemic Awareness is an awareness of individual sounds in spoken language and the ability to manipulate those sounds.)

▣ 중요성

아이들이 읽기에 성공하려면 단어가 어떤 소리로 구성되어 있는지 반드시 알아야 한다. 또한 Phonemic Awareness가 부족한 아이의 경우 차후에 읽기 과정에서 문제가 발생한다는 연구가 보고되기도 했다. 게다가 Phonemic Awareness는 차후에 배울 Phonics 학습의 기초가 되기 때문에 매우 중요하다.

▣ 지도 방법

Phonemic Awareness의 주요 학습 내용은 다음과 같다.

- 개별 음소 알기(Identify phonemes)
  T : What sound is the same in ball, boy, and bed?
  (ball, boy, bed에서 공통된 소리는 무엇인가요?)
- 음소 합치기(Blend phonemes to form words)
  T : What word is /s/ /u/ /n/?
  (/s/ /u/ /n/은 어떤 단어가 되나요?)
- 음소 나누기(Segment words into phonemes)
  T : How many sounds are in desk?
  (desk란 단어에는 몇 개의 소리가 있나요?)
- 음소 더하기, 없애기, 바꾸기(Add, delete, and substitute phonemes)
  T : What word do you have if you add /s/ to the beginning of top?
  (top이란 단어에 /s/를 더하면 어떤 단어가 되나요?)

T : What word is plate without the /p/?
(plate란 단어에서 /p/를 없애면 어떤 단어가 되나요?)

T : If you start with the word pet and change /t/ to /n/ what is the new word?
(pet이란 단어에서 /t/ 대신 /n/으로 바꾸면 어떤 단어가 되나요?)

▣ 수업의 예

T : The word 'cat' can be broken up into parts. Breaking words into parts can help us to read words. I think we can break this word up easily.
Jenny, would you like to try?
('cat' 이란 단어는 둘로 쪼갤 수 있어요. 단어를 쪼개면 단어 읽기가 훨씬 쉽죠. 이 단어를 쪼개볼까요? 제니, 해볼래요?)

S : If you take away the c and leave that /a/ /t/, it would be at.
(/a/ /t/를 남기고 c를 없애면 at가 되요.)

T : That's right. If you take away the c and leave the /a/ /t/, it would be at. So you found a part of the word. Which part of the word did she find, the first part or the last part? Kenny?
(맞았어요. /a/ /t/를 남기고 c를 없애면 at가 되지요. 그래서 단어의 부분을 알았네요. 제니가 찾은 단어는 첫 부분인가요 끝부분인가요? 케니?)

S : The last part.
(끝부분이에요.)

T : Good job. She found the last part. Let's take a look at the first part. Let's break that word up into /c/ /at/. The first part is /c/(claps as she says sound). Okay, we have /c/ for the first part, and here we clap, The second part is /at/, so we slap. Now watch me – /c/ (clap) /at/ (slap). Cat. Now you try it.
(잘했어요. 제니가 찾은 것은 끝부분이에요. 이제 첫 부분을 봅시다. 이 단어는 /c/ /at/로 되어 있어요. 첫 부분은 /c/(교사는 소리를 내면서 박수를 친다.)
자, 첫 부분인 /c/에선 우리는 박수를 칩니다. 두 번째 부분 /at/에서는 손바닥을 내리친다. 선생님을 보세요. /c/ 박수, /at/ 손바닥 내리치기. cat. 여러분이 해보세요.)

S : /c/(clap)/at/(slap). Cat.
(/c/ 박수, /at/ 손바닥 내리치기. cat.)

⊙ 파닉스(Phonics)

▣ 정의

파닉스(Phonics)란 소리와 철자와의 관계이다. (Phonics is the relationship between speech sounds and their spellings.)

▣ 중요성

철자와 소리와의 관계를 제대로 이해하게 되면 단어를 정확하게 읽을 수 있고, 새로운 단어를 보더라도 쉽게 읽을 수 있다.

▣ 지도 방법

Phonics는 체계적(systematic)이고 명확하게(explicit) 지도할 때 가장 효과적이다.

- 체계적인 학습(A systematic program)
  자음과 모음을 포함한 소리와 철자의 관계를 체계적으로 학습한다.
- 명확한 학습(A explicit program)
  교사는 철자와 소리에 관한 지식을 가지고 어떻게 읽고, 쓸 수 있는지 명확하게 가르친다.

▣ 수업의 예

T : I am going to read the book for the first time and you are going to listen. Then the second time you are going to help me by doing some searching. Your focus will be to find rhyming words and decide if they have the same or different spelling patterns. Sometimes two words rhyme, and even though they sound alike, they may not be spelled alike. I' m going to show you what I mean with example. See and me are rhyming words. Do they sound like?
(책을 처음 읽을 건데, 잘 들으세요. 그리고 두 번째 읽을 때는 무언가를 찾을텐데, 여러분이 도와주세요. 우리는 rhyming words를 찾을 건데요, 철자패턴이 같을 수도 혹은 다를 수도 있어요. 경우에 따라서 두 단어가 라임이 같으면, 소리는 같게 나도, 철자가 다를 수 있어요. 예를 들면 see와 me란 단어는 rhyming words죠. 두 단어가 소리가 같나요?)

S : Yes. (네)

T : Yes. But loot at them. Look at the way they are spelled. What do you notice?
(네, 하지만 잘 보세요. 철자는 다르네요. 어떻게 다른가요?)

S : That see has two es and me has only one e.
(See는 e가 두 개고, me는 e가 하나에요.)

T : Right. so the spelling pattern, or word family, at the end is spelled differently. Today as you listen to the story, you are going to search for rhyming words. Then we have to decide if those rhyming words have the same word family or different word families. First listen to the story.
(네, 그래서 철자 패턴 혹은 word family는 끝이 철자가 다르기도 해요. 오늘은 이야기를 들으면서, rhyming words를 찾으세요. 그런 후에 rhyming words 가 같은 word family 인지 아닌지 결정해야 해요. 먼저 이야기를 들어보세요.)

⊙ 유창성(Fluency)

▣ 정의

유창성(Fluency)이란 글을 정확하게 빠르게 읽는 능력을 말하며, Fluent Reader는 어떤 표현으로 읽어야 하는지 알며, 동시에 의미도 이해하며 문장을 읽는다. (Fluency is the ability to read text quickly accurately with comprehension and expression.)

▣ 중요성

단어를 쉽게 해독하고, 어디에서 끊어 읽고, 어디에서 멈추며, 적절한 억양으로 읽게 되면 훨씬 더 글을 이해하기 쉽다.

■ 지도 방법

다음의 두 가지 방법으로 아이들은 fluent reader가 될 수 있다.

• 모델 수업(Model fluent reading)
  교사가 시범적으로 읽기 하는 모습을 보여주고, 아이들은 똑같이 따라서 연습한다.

• 가이드 수업(Guide oral reading)
  40~200단어로 된 짧은 글을 아이들에게 읽게 시킨 후, 교사와 부모가 가이드와 피드백을 준다.

■ 수업의 예

T : Listen to how I read the first sentence of the story: "The wind bleeew." What did you notice about the way I read that sentence?
(선생님이 이야기의 첫 문장을 어떻게 읽는지 들어보세요. "The wind bleeew." 내가 어떤 방식으로 문장을 읽었는지 알겠어요?)

S : You made the word blew sound long.
(단어 blew를 길게 발음했어요.)

T : That's right. I stretched out the sound in the word. Why do you think I did that?
(맞았어요. 단어를 길게 늘여서 소리 냈어요. 왜 그렇게 했을까요?)

S : To make the story more interesting.
(이야기를 더 재미있게 하기 위해서요.)

T : True, I wanted to make the words sound interesting. But why do you think I chose to read the word blew the way I did?
(맞아요. 단어를 재미있게 소리 내고 싶었어요. 그런데, blew란 단어를 그런 방식으로 읽었을까요?)

S : Maybe to sort of sound like the wind?
(아마 바람 소리와 비슷하게 하기 위해서인가요?)

T : You got it! How does the wind sound when it blows?
(그래요. 바람이 불 때 어떤 소리가 나지요?)

S : Whhhhhhhhh.
(위~)

T : Now say "bleeeeeeew."
("bleeeeeeew."라고 말해봅시다.)

S : "bleeeeeeew."

T : When we stretch out the sounds in the word blew, it sounds a little like the stretched out sound of wind blowing. Now we can more easily picture the windy, windy day that is describe in this story.
(blew란 단어를 길게 소리 내면, 바람이 불어오는 소리 같아요. 이제 좀 더 쉽게 이야기에서 묘사하고 있는 바람 부는 날을 그릴 수가 있어요.)

S : I think reading blew like "bleeeeeeew." tells that is really, really, really windy.
(blew를 "bleeeeeeew."로 읽으면서 정말 정말 정말 심하게 바람이 부는 거라고 생각했어요.)

T : Great point. Look at the picture. This isn' t just a breezy day. This looks like a very, very windy day. And if I read you this first sentence the way that I did, but I didn' t show you the picture, you would have a better understanding that the wind was a strong wind. Listen to the way I read sentence once again and they you echo the way I read it : "The wind bleeeew."
(훌륭한 지적이에요. 그림을 보세요. 살랑살랑 바람이 부는 게 아니에요. 이건 정말 매우 심하게 바람이 부는 날이에요. 그래서 내가 이 첫 문장을 이렇게 읽어주고, 여러분에게 그림을 보여주지 않았지만, 여러분은 바람이 아주 강하다는 걸 이해 할 수 있었어요. 내가 한 번 더 문장을 읽을 테니, 여러분은 따라 읽으세요. "The wind bleeeew.")

S : "The wind bleeeew."

⊙ 어휘(Vocabulary)

▣ 정의

어휘(Vocabulary)란 우리가 효과적으로 의사소통을 하기 위해서 반드시 알아야 할 단어를 말한다. (Vocabulary is a group of words we must know to communicate effectively.)

▣ 중요성

글을 읽을 때 단어의 의미를 모른다면, 글을 이해하는데 문제가 된다.

▣ 지도 방법

단어 지도 방법은 간접 지도 방법과 직접 지도 방법 두 가지가 있다.

- 간접 지도 방법(Indirect vocabulary learning)
  아이들에게 말할 기회를 많이 준다. 자주 책을 읽어주고, 책에 관해 이야기해준다.
  아이들 스스로가 책을 읽을 수 있도록 격려한다.

- 직접 지도 방법(Direct vocabulary learning)
  책을 읽기 전에 미리 단어를 가르친다. 다양한 글에서 단어를 발췌하여 가르친다.
  사전을 사용하는 방법을 가르친다. 단어에 관한 지식을 가르친다.

▣ 수업의 예

Word Parts를 쉽게 익힐 수 있는 방법

Word – Ending Flowers

여섯 개의 꽃잎이 있는 꽃을 그린다. 꽃의 가운데에, base word를 쓰고, 꽃잎에 suffixes, prefixes, 혹은 이것을 합한 단어를 쓴다. 접두사나 접미사가 붙어서 단어의 뜻이 어떻게 변했는지 이야기 나눈다. 각 단어가 들어가는 문장을 만든 후, 꽃잎 옆에 문장을 적는다.

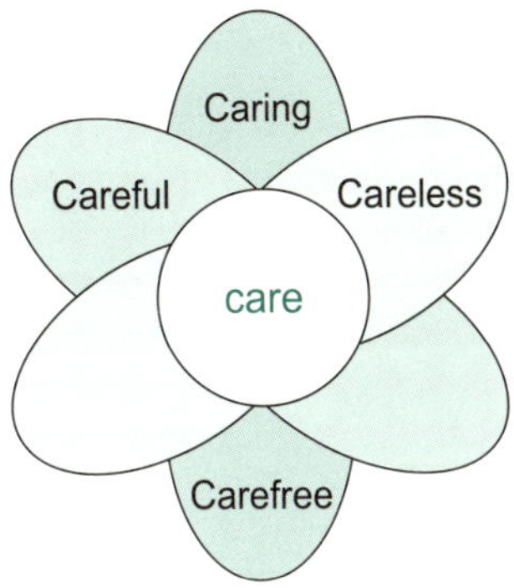

– You have to be ***careful.***

⊙ 이해(Comprehension)

▣ 정의

이해(Comprehension)란 읽고 있는 글의 내용의 의미를 아는 것이다. (Comprehension is understanding the meaning of what is read.)

▣ 중요성

이 과정을 통해 아이들은 책을 읽을 때 다양한 목적을 가지게 되고, 글을 이해하기 위해 자신의 경험과 읽기 전략을 사용할 줄 아는 적극적인 독자가 된다.

▣ 지도 방법

효과적으로 글을 이해 할 수 있는 6가지의 전략은 다음과 같다.

- 이해도 모니터하기(Monitoring Comprehension)
  이해한 것과 이해하지 못한 것을 아이들 스스로 안다.
- 그래픽 오거나이저(Graphic organizers)
  글의 내용을 도표 등을 활용하여 시각화 한다.

- 질문하고 대답하기(Answering questions)

  어떤 목적을 가지고 읽기를 하는지, 읽는 동안 활발하게 생각은 하고 있는지, 이해도를 체크하고 있는지, 아이들이 배운 내용과 사전지식을 연결시키게 도와준다.

- 질문 만들기(Generating questions)

  아이들이 글을 이해했는지 질문을 한다.

- 이야기 구조 인지하기(Recognizing story structure)

  이야기를 이해하고, 기억하기위해 사건(event)을 분류하고, 구성(plot)을 분석한다.

- 요약하기(Summarizing)

  이야기의 흐름을 파악하여 기억할 수 있게 주요한 정보를 요약한다.

▣ 수업의 예

Graphic organizers를 활용한 수업

T : During the first reading your are listening, you are thinking. The second time, we are going to fill in this chart with the informations in this book. Did you know that this chart is called a graphic organizer? Those are very grown up words, but a graphic organizer helps us organize information. here we go.

(처음 읽을 때 여러분은 잘 들으면서, 생각을 해요. 두 번째 읽고 나서는 이 책에서 얻은 정보를 가지고 이 차트를 채울 겁니다. 이 차트를 graphic organizer라고 부른다는 걸 아나요? 이 단어는 어른용 단어지만, graphic organizer는 정보를 조직화하는데 도움을 줍니다. 시작해 볼까요?

「*How Puppies Grow*」의 Graphic organizer

How Puppies Grow

by Millicent E.Selsam

⇨

One Week Old

can	can not
taste touch suck milk eat sleep crawl around	see hear

⇨

Two Weeks Old

- Tries to walk but falls
- Eyes are opening
- Can see some things

⇩

Four Weeks Old

- Walks without falling
- Sees better
- Hears sounds
- Has some teeth
- Eats solid food
- Still needs mom's milk
- Play with mom

⇦

Seven Week Old

- Runs, chases, tumbles, plays all the time.
- Is learning to do without mom's milk
- Eats more and more solid food
- Mom leaves them alone more

⇦

T : What did you learn from this graphic organizer?
(graphic organizer에서 무엇을 배웠나요?)

S : It helps you to remember everything.
(모든 것을 기억하기 쉽게 해줘요.)

T : Yes. It helps you remember information, and also to put the information in the right order. Also, This chart is good because it helps me organize information by time. Other graphic organizers helps me tell a story with a beginning, middle, or end, or compare two characters. There are lots of ways to organize information with graphic organizers.
(그래요. 정보를 쉽게 기억할 수 있게 하고, 또 정보를 순서대로 맞출 수도 있어요. 또 이 차트가 좋은 이유는 시간 순서대로 정보를 조직화 할 수 있다는 겁니다. 다른 graphic organizer는 시작, 중간, 끝을 알려주기도 하고, 두 인물을 비교해주기도 해요. graphic organizer로 정보를 조직화하는 여러 방법이 있지요.)

Graphic organizers

다음은 이해(comprehension)를 도울 수 있는 그래픽 오거나이저(Graphic organizers)다.

Story Map

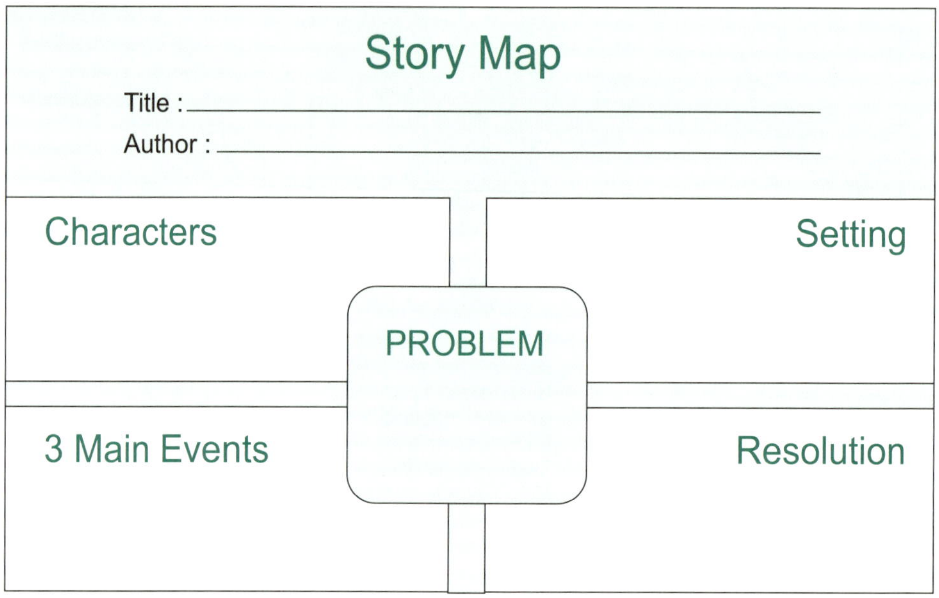

Character Map

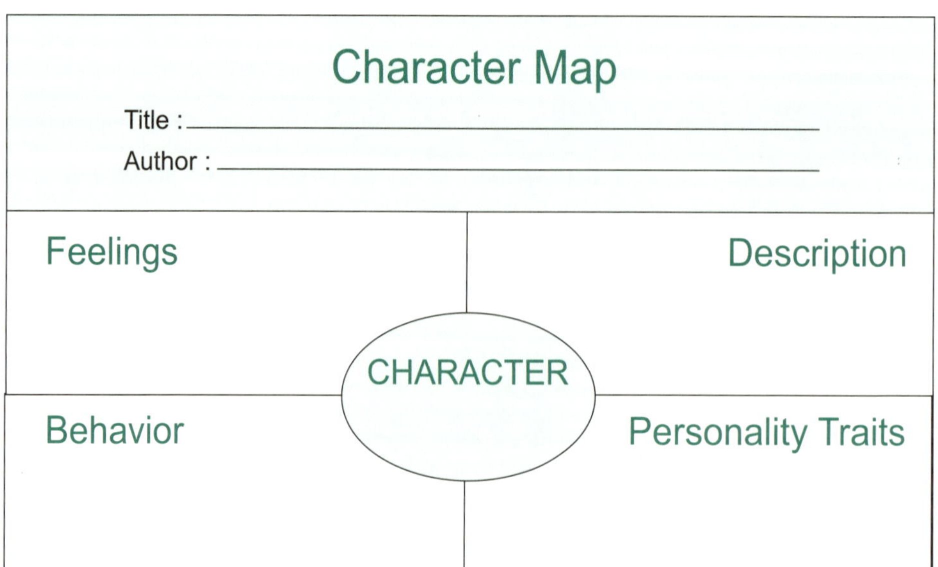

Cause and Effect

Why Did It Happen?

Think about an event or a character's action that you read about. Then write what happened as a result of this.

This is title of what I read : ______________________________

This is the cause statement :		Here are the effects :
______________________ ______________________ ______________________ Draw a picture to show the cause.	⇨	______________________ ______________________ ______________________ Draw a picture to show the effect.

Sequencing

Tell the Story

In what order did the events happen? Topic : ____________________

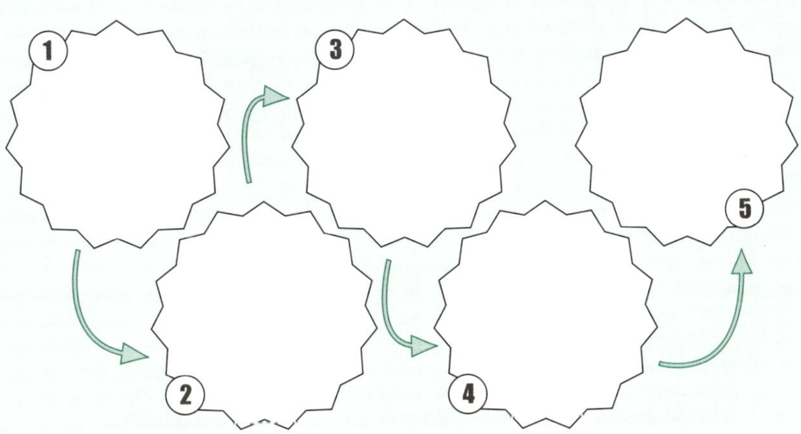

2 읽기 과정(Reading Process)

읽기 과정(Reading Process)이란 다음의 5 단계를 차례대로 밟아가면서 활동을 하는 것을 말한다. 각 과정에 대해 상세하게 알아보자.

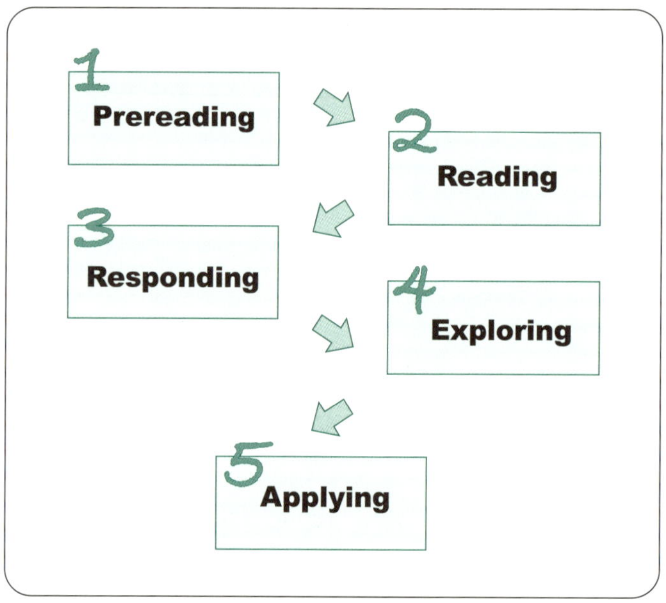

1) 읽기 준비하기(Prereading)

읽기의 시작은 책을 펴서 첫 문장을 읽는 것에서 시작되는 것이 아니다. 읽기의 첫 단계는 읽을 준비를 하는 것이다. 구체적인 활동으로는 아이들의 배경지식(background knowledge)을 모으고, 책 읽는 목적을 정하고, 읽기를 어떻게 진행할지 계획을 세우는 것이 이 과정에 속한다.

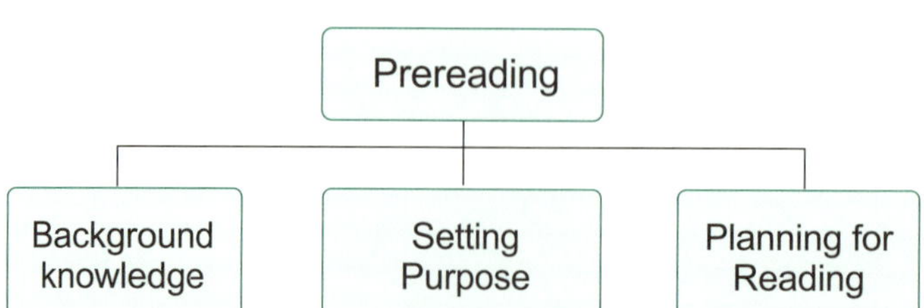

■ 배경지식 (Background Knowledge)

아이에게 책의 내용과 관련된 것에 대해 비슷한 경험을 하거나, 혹은 이와 유사한 동화를 읽었거나 (혹은 유사한 이야기를 들은 경우도 해당 된다.), 같은 작가의 또 다른 작품에 대해 이야기 나눠보는 것이 바로 배경지식(background knowledge)을 모으는 것이다. 만약 선택한 동화의 내용이 아이들에게 매우 생소할 경우에는 책의 선택을 재고해 보거나, 아니면 책을 이해할 수 있는데 필요한 배경지식을 얻을 수 있도록 많은 자료들을 준비해야 한다. 예를 들어 선택한 책이 농장에 관한 것인데, 아이들 모두 농장에 한 번도 가 본 적이 없다면, 농장 사진과 농장에 사는 동물 그림 등을 준비해서 간접 경험의 시간을 주어야 한다. 배경지식(background knowledge)과 비슷한 용어로는 사전 지식(prior knowledge), 또는 스키마 (schema)가 있다. 이들 세 용어의 의미는 같다고 보면 된다. 그렇다면 배경지식이 왜 중요할까? 그 이유는 읽기를 할 때에 필요한 사전 지식을 갖추어야만 작가가 의도한 것을 제대로 이해할 수 있기 때문이다. 따라서 모든 영어 동화 지도의 첫 단계는 바로 어떤 배경지식을 활용할 지 결정하는 것이 중요하다. 자, 그렇다면 배경지식을 모으는 방법에 대해 알아보자.

배경지식 모으는 방법(How to Build Background Knowledge)	
사진, 그림, 실물 보여주기 (Show photos, pictures, real things.) 	수 천 마디의 말보다 한 장의 그림이나, 실물을 보여주는 것이 효과적이다. 인터넷이나 각종 시각적 자료를 준비해서 아이들에게 보여주어야 한다. 예를 들어 할로윈(Halloween)에 집 밖에 장식을 하는 호박등불(Jack-o'-lantern)에 관한 수업을 한다면 사진 혹은 실물의 호박등불을 보여주는 것이 가장 효과적이다.

경험 나누기 (Share Experience)  	Share Experience는 말 그대로 아이들의 경험을 나누어 보는 시간을 갖는 것이다. 「*Five Little Monkeys Jumping on the Bed*」로 예를 들어 보자. T : What are they doing now? Right, They are jumping on the bed. Have you been jumping on the bed? I know it can make you fun. But I think it might be very dangerous for you to jump on the bed. You can fall off and bump your head. (원숭이들이 무엇을 하고 있나요? 그래요, 침대에서 뛰고 있어요. 여러분도 침대 위에서 뛰어 본 경험이 있나요? 침대에서 뛰는 것은 신나는 일이죠. 하지만 침대에서 뛰는 것은 매우 위험한 일이에요. 침대에서 뛰다가 떨어져서, 머리를 다칠 수도 있어요.)
관련된 글 제시하기 (Related Text) 	Related Text란 교사가 고른 영어동화책을 읽어 주기 전에 이와 관련된 글을 제시해 주는 것을 말한다. 예를 들어 「*Brown Bear Brown Bear What do you see?*」란 동화를 읽어 주기 전에 아래의 「*Bears*」란 시를 미리 제시하여 주는 것이다. 영어동화의 대부분이 주로 산문으로 되어 있기 때문에, 관련된 글을 읽어 줄 때는 산문이 아닌 시(Poetry)로 된 것을 읽어 주는 것도 좋다. *Bears* Large bears Small bears Watch the bears grow. Tall chairs Small chairs Watch the bears eat. Long beds Shorts beds Watch the bears take a nap. Loud bears Quiet bears Watch the bears wake up.

<table>
<tr><td>브레인스토밍
(Brainstorming)
</td><td>Brainstorming은 1939년에 미국의 광고회사 부사장 A. F. 오즈번이 제창하여 그의 저서 「독창력을 신장하라(1953)」를 통해 널리 알려진 방법으로, '두뇌'라는 뜻의 'brain'과 '폭풍'이라는 뜻의 'storming'이 결합된 단어로 여러 사람이 모여서 빠른 시간에 많은 아이디어를 내는 아이디어 발상법을 말한다. 다음은 브레인스토밍을 할 때 지켜야 할 규칙을 정리한 것이다.
• 어떠한 내용의 발언이라도 그에 대한 비판을 해서는 안 된다.
• 옳고 그름, 좋고 나쁨을 따지지 않는다.
• 자유분방하고 엉뚱하기까지 한 의견도 받아들인다.
• 아이디어 수가 많을수록 좋다.
• 나온 아이디어를 메모한다.</td></tr>
<tr><td>아는 것 -
궁금한 것 -
배운 것
(K - W - L)차트
</td><td>KWL차트는 사선지식을 일깨우기 위해 가장 흔하게 사용되는 방법으로, 크게 세 칸으로 분리되는데, 첫 번째 칸 What do I Know? 에는 아이들이 이미 알고 있는 지식을 적고, 두 번째 칸 What do I Want to know? 에는 아이들이 알고 싶어하는 내용을 적는다. 마지막 칸 What did I Learn? 은 조사가 다 끝난 후에 적는다. 이 차트를 이용하여 아이들은 자신들이 배우고 있는 내용의 의미를 깨닫고 자신이 이미 알고 있었던 지식과 새로운 지식을 비교하며 자신의 생각을 분명하게 정립시키게 된다. 예로 「Owl Babies」 수업을 할 경우, 수업 전에 올빼미에 관한 정보를 모아보고, 앞으로 올빼미에 대해서 무엇이 궁금한지를 정리해 본다.
T : Can you tell me something about owls? Sure. They have very big eyes and wings, and a sharp beak and claws.
(올빼미에 대해서 말해 줄래? 좋아요. 큰 눈과 큰 날개, 날카로운 부리와 발톱을 가지고 있어요.)
T : What do they eat? They eat small animals and insects.
(무엇을 먹니? 작은 동물들과 곤충들이요.)</td></tr>
</table>

<table>
<tr>
<td>아는 것－
궁금한 것－
배운 것
(K－W－L)차트</td>
<td>T : Where do they live? They live in trees.
(어디에 사는지 아니? 올빼미는 나무에 살지요.)

T : When do they catch their food, during the day or night?
(먹이는 언제 잡니? 낮에, 밤에?)

S : They catch their food during the night.
(밤에요.)

T : You really know a lot about owls. Now, let's write what we know now about owls in this column.
(정말 올빼미에 대해서 많이 알고 있구나. 올빼미에 대해서 알고 있는 것을 이 칸에 적어 보자.)

<table>
<tr><th>K</th><th>W</th><th>L</th></tr>
<tr><td>What do you think you KNOW about Owls?</td><td>What do you WANT to know about Owls?</td><td>What do you LEARN about Owls?</td></tr>
<tr><td></td><td></td><td></td></tr>
</table>
</td>
</tr>
<tr>
<td>예측하기
(Predicting)
</td>
<td>Predict에서 'pre'는 '먼저'라는 뜻이고, 'dict'는 '말하다'라는 뜻으로 'predict'는 '미리 말하다'라는 뜻이다. 그렇다면 Before Reading 단계에서 무엇을 미리 말해야 할까? 영어 동화책의 경우에는 우선 책의 표지에 있는 그림(the cover illustration)과 책의 제목(the title of new book)을 아이들에게 보여준 후, 동화의 이야기가 어떻게 펼쳐질 것인지 아이들에게 예측하게 해서 미리 말하게 한다.</td>
</tr>
</table>

<table>
<tr><td>예측하기
(Predicting)</td><td>T : Look at this cover! What will happen in the story? I'll give you some hints. The children are showing their hands. What do you think they want to tell us?
(표지를 보세요. 어떤 일이 벌어질까요? 힌트를 줄게요. 아이들이 모두 손을 보여주고 있네요. 아이들이 무슨 이야기를 하려고 할까요?)

S : I got it. I think they want to talk about their hands. And I see the word 'hands' in the title.
(손에 관한 이야기를 할 것 같아요. 또 제목에도 hands란 단어가 있네요.)</td></tr>
<tr><td>작가에 관해
이야기 하기
(Talk about
an author or
illustrator)

</td><td>같은 작가의 여러 동화책을 배웠다면 그 작가만이 가진 특징에 관해 이야기 해보는 것도 좋나. 예를 늘어 Eric Carle의 경우 애벌레나 거미, 귀뚜라미처럼 작은 벌레가 주인공으로 자주 등장하는데, 왜 그런지 그 이유를 알아보고, Eric Carle의 작품 중에 작은 벌레를 소재로 다룬 동화에는 무엇이 있는지 알아보는 활동도 작가의 작품을 예측해볼 수 있는 방법 중의 하나이다.

T : Why does Eric Carle use small creatures in his books most of the time? Let's read his answer.
(왜 Eric Carle은 작은 생물을 책의 소재로 썼을까? 그의 대답을 읽어 보자.)

Eric Carle's Answer :
When I was a small boy, my father would take me on walks across meadows and through woods. He would lift a stone or peel back the bark of a tree and show me the living things that scurried about. He'd tell me about the life cycles of this or that small creature and then he would carefully put the little creature back into its home. I think in my books I honor my father by writing about small living things. And in a way I recapture those happy times.
http://www.eric-carle.com/bio.html(Eric Carle 홈페이지)</td></tr>
</table>

■ 목표 세우기(Setting Purpose)

Prereading 단계에서 가장 중요한 것은 목적 세우기(setting the purpose for reading)이다. 앞서 설명한 다양한 방법으로 배경지식을 모으는 이유도 읽기의 목적을 정하기 위한 것이다. 이러한 책 읽기 목적은 크게 두 가지로 나눌 수 있다. 하나는 즐거움(pleasure)이고, 또 하나는 정보(information)를 얻기 위해서다. 예를 들어 「*The Rainbow Fish*」란 동화로 수업을 할 때, 교사가 가장 먼저 생각해야 하는 것은 이 책을 내가 왜 선택했는지, 그 목적을 분명히 정해야 한다. 단순히 언어의 재미를 주기 위해서인지, 아니면 물에 사는 물고기에 대해 가르치기 위해선지, 아니면 나눔(share)에 대해 알려주기 위한 것인지 책을 읽는 목적을 분명히 정해야 한다. 그래야 그 목적에 따라 수업계획을 세울 수 있기 때문이다. 또 목표를 정하고 책을 읽으면 읽기의 방향을 잡아나가기 쉬울 뿐만 아니라, 스스로 제대로 읽고 나가고 있는지 체크를 하기 편하다. 따라서 교사나 아이들 모두 책을 읽을 때는 내가 이 책을 왜 읽는지 그 목표부터 정확하고 구체적으로 세워야 한다.

■ 읽기 계획 세우기(Planning for Reading)

아이들은 책을 본격적으로 읽기 전에 책의 길이, 목차, 삽화, 차트 등을 한번 쭉 훑어본다. 이렇게 책을 미리 보면서 자신이 가진 배경지식을 어떻게 활용할지, 왜 책을 읽어야하는지 목표도 확인하게 된다. 특히 정보를 얻기 위한 정보 책 (information book)을 읽을 때는 학습일지(learning log)를 작성하는 것도 매우 좋은 활동이다.

■ 학습일지(Learning Log)

학습일지(learning log) 란 수업시간에 배운 내용에 자신의 생각을 첨가해서 글을 쓰는 것으로 학습을 적극적이고 책임감 있게 수용하도록 훈련시킬 수 있는 효과적인 학습방법이다. 아이들은 학습일지를 씀으로써 자신이 수업시간에 배웠던 내용이 무엇이었는가를 정리할 수 있으며 또한 배운 내용과 관계되는 다양한 새로운 문제들과 질문들을 제기함으로써 학습의 과정을 창의적이고, 비판적이며, 적극적인 것으로 발전시키도록 도와 준다.

Learning Log

Name: : ____________________ Date : ________________________

Name of Report :

Purpose/Object of Report :

What I did :

What I learned :

How I could improve my reporting skills :

Teacher Comments :

2) 읽기(Reading)

읽기의 두 번째 단계는 책을 펴서 읽는 것으로 이 때, 글을 제대로 이해하기 위해서 자신이 가진 모든 지식을 총동원하게 되는데, 만일 읽은 내용이 이해가 가지 않을 경우에는 천천히 읽거나, 다시 읽거나, 혹은 앞으로 되돌아가서 글을 읽게 된다.

교실에서 일어날 수 있는 읽기의 유형은 크게 다섯 가지(independent reading, buddy reading, guided reading, shared reading, reading aloud)이다. 각각의 읽기 유형에 대해 간략하게 알아보자.

유 형	특 징
Independent Reading	학생들이 혼자서 글을 읽는다. 책임감과 소유욕을 키울 수 있다. 스스로 책을 선택해서 읽는다. 진정한 책읽기 경험이다. 교사의 참여와 통제가 거의 없다.
Buddy Reading	두 명의 학생이 함께 읽는다. 학생들 사이에 협동심이 생긴다. 유창하게 읽을 수 있게 도움이 된다. 이미 배워서 친숙한 글을 읽을 때 좋은 유형이다. 학생들은 자신이 해석한 내용을 서로 이야기하면서 의견을 나눈다.
Guided Reading	교사의 지도하에 학생이 읽기전략과 기술을 적용해 가면서 글을 읽는다. 교사는 올바르게 책 읽는 방법과 전략을 제시한다. 혼자서 읽기에는 힘든 글을 읽을 때 좋은 유형이다.
Shared Reading	교사는 빅 북(big book)을 읽어 주고, 학생은 개인별로 책을 가지고 있어서, 교사가 읽어 주는 내용을 따라 가며 읽는다. 교사는 유창하게 읽는 모습을 보여주고, 학생은 유창하게 읽기 연습을 한다. 읽기를 같이 하면서 협동심을 키울 수 있다.

Reading aloud	교사가 학생들에게 책을 읽어 준다. 학생이 스스로 읽을 수 없는 책을 읽어 준다. 교사 혼자서 책을 가지고 읽어 준다. 교사는 책을 읽을 때 어떻게 읽는지 모델을 제시한다.

3) 반응하기(Responding)

읽기 과정의 세 번째 단계인 반응하기(responding)는 책을 읽으면서 그 의미를 제대로 이해하는지 질문을 하고 그에 대해 답을 하는 것을 말한다. 이 과정에서 쓸 수 있는 가장 효과적인 방법은 토론(grand conversation)을 하는 것과 읽기 일지(reading log)를 작성하는 것이다.

■ 토론하기 (Grand Conversation)

Grand Conversation이란 책을 읽고 나서 느낌이나 생각한 것에 대해 토론하는 것을 말한다. 이 때는 아이들은 서로 얼굴을 볼 수 있도록 둥근 형태로 앉는 것이 좋다. 이 때 교사는 토론을 활발하게 이끌어가기 위한 보조자 역할을 한다. 이 때 앞서 제시한 읽기 일지를 활용해도 된다. 토론 진행 순서는 먼저 책을 읽고 나서, 아이들은 각자 자신의 생각을 정리하게 한다. 때로 이 과정은 생략할 수도 있다. 그런 후 교사는 책의 내용을 제대로 이해했는지 질문을 던져 봄으로써, 아이들의 이해도를 점검한다. 다음은 이와 관련된 질문 내용이다.

> Who are the main characters?(주인공은 누구인가요?)
> What is the setting?(배경은 어딘가요?)
> When does this story take place?(이야기가 일어난 시간은 언제인가요?)
> Is this story fact or fiction?(이야기는 사실인가요 아니면 허구인가요?)

그런 후, 책에 관해서 열린 토론을 한다. 이 때 교사는 어떤 부분이 좋았는지, 책을 읽으면서 어떤 생각을 했는지와 같은 질문을 던진다. 교사의 질문에 아이들은 대답을 해가면서 서로의 생각을 공유한다. 토론을 끝낸 후에 토론이 어떠했는지 평가하는 시간을 갖으면서 마무리한다.

■ 읽기 일지(Reading Log)

아이들은 자신이 읽은 글에 대해 생각이나 느낌을 글로 쓰거나, 그림을 그려서 일지를 쓰게 된다. 다음은 다양한 형태의 읽기 일지(reading log) 샘플이다.

Reading Log						
Title	Date Started	Date Finished	Characters	Setting	Conflicts	Ending

Accelerated Reader Summer Reading Log			
Date	Auther	Title	What I liked about the book

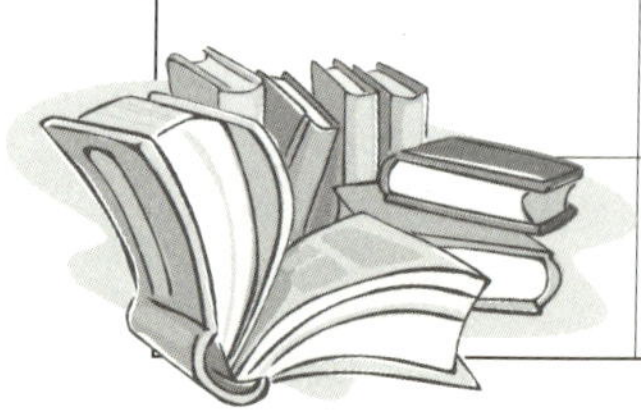

Name : ______________________

MY Reading Log

	Date	Title	Author	Minutes	Parent Signature
01					
02					
03					
04					
05					
06					
07					
08					
09					
10					
11					
12					
13					
14					
15					

Pick Me!!

Anything can happen...
When you open a book!

또 다른 형태로는 일년 동안 읽은 목록을 한 파일에 정리하는 방법이 있다. 1월부터 시작해서, 12월까지 매달 읽은 책을 다달이 정리하는 방법으로, 다음의 그림 자료를 참고하기 바란다.

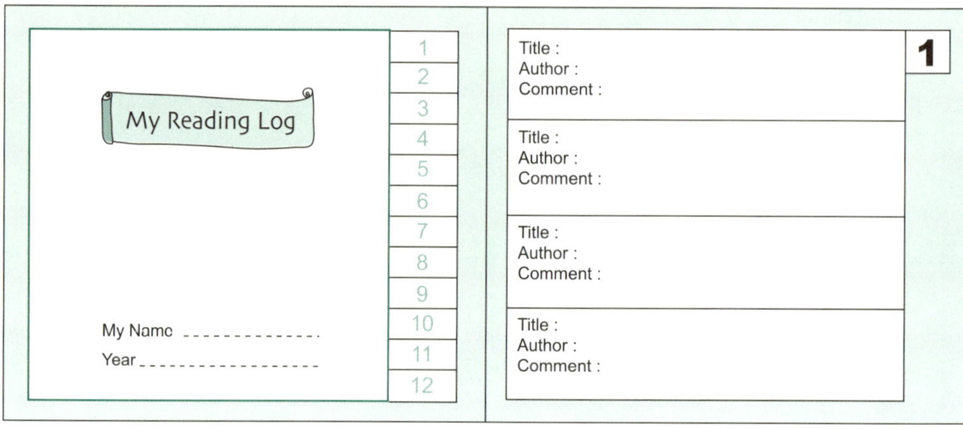

4) 탐험하기(Exploring)

읽기 과정의 네 번째 단계인 Exploring은 책을 좀 더 분석적으로 탐험하는 것으로, 이 과정에서는 교사가 주축이 되어서 활동을 하게 된다. Exploring 활동은 크게 세 가지로 나눌 수 있다.

※ 선별적 다시 읽기(Rereading the Selection)

읽은 책의 일부분을 선별해서 다시 읽는 것을 말한다. 부모와 혹은 친구와 같이 읽거나, Shared Reading 시간에 교사와 다시 한 번 읽으면서, 자신의 삶과 연결시키거나, 예전에 읽었던 책과 연결시켜 보는 활동을 한다. 이 과정을 통해서 차후에 혼자 읽기가 가능해진다.

※ 작가 연구하기(Examining the Author)

작가 특유의 언어적 특징이나 그림 특징에 초점을 맞추어서 활동을 한다. 책의 일부분을 선별해서 그 부분을 아이들이 자신만의 언어로 새롭게 글을 쓰기도 하는데, 책의 결론을 바꾸거나, 이야기가 끝난 후에 주인공이 어떻게 변화되었는지에 대한 글을 쓰기도 한다.

※ 단어와 문장에 초점 맞추기(Focusing and Words and Sentence)

책의 글에서 익혀야 할 중요 단어와 문장을 뽑는다. 이 때 선별한 단어를 가지고 파닉스 수업을 하면서, 단어에 대해 심도 있게 수업을 한다. 또 핵심이 되는 문장을 골라서 다시 읽기를 하거나, 아이들에게 문장을 베껴 쓰게 한다. 이 문장은 독서일지(reading log)에 옮겨 적게 한다.

5) 적용하기(Applying)

마지막 단계 적용하기(applying)에서는 아이들이 자신이 이해한 것을 확장시키는 단계로, 책을 읽으면서 이해한 것에 대해 곰곰이 생각해 보기도 하고, 책읽기 경험에 대한 평가를 내리기도 한다. 이 때 아이들에게 프로젝트를 주어서 마무리하기도 하는데, 보고서를 작성하거나, 연극을 하거나, 같은 작가의 다른 작품을 읽으면서 작품 비교를 하기도 한다. 이 외의 프로젝트 활동은 다음과 같다.

적용하기 과정의 프로젝트(Project During the Applying Stage)
시각적 프로젝트(Visual Projects) • 책에서 얻은 정보를 활용해서 다이어그램 만들기 • 중요 사건을 그림으로 그려보기 • 가장 인상 깊었던 장면을 그림으로 그려보기
읽기 프로젝트(Reading Projects) • 같은 작가의 다른 책 읽어 보기 • 같은 주제로 된 다른 책 읽어 보기 • 같은 장르의 다른 책 보기 • 같은 주인공이 나오는 다른 책 읽어 보기 • 책에서 가장 인상 깊은 장면을 선정해서 녹음기에 녹음해 보기
검색 프로젝트(Research Projects) • 작가의 책을 인터넷에서 검색하고, 정보를 수집하여 목록을 만든다. • 책의 주제와 관련된 내용을 검색하여 보고서를 만든다.
드라마와 이야기 프로젝트(Drama and Talk Projects) • 주인공이 입었던 옷을 입고, 아이들과 어떤 주인공인지 알아맞추기를 한다. • 책을 팔기 위해 상업용 비디오테이프를 만들어 본다. • 책의 주제에 대해 지식이 풍부한 사람을 찾아 인터뷰한다. • 읽은 책을 연극할 수 있는 대본을 쓴다.

다음은 「Three Little Pigs」의 연극 대본이다.

Three Little Pigs

[등장인물: Narrator, Pig 1, Pig 2, Pig 3, Wolf]

Narrator : Once upon a time there were three little pigs. They were each going to make a house to live in.

Pig 1 : I will make a house of straw.

Pig 2 : I will make a house of sticks.

Pig 3 : I will make a house of bricks.

Narrator : The wolf goes to the house of the first little pig.

Wolf : Little pig, little pig, let me come in!

Pig 1 : Not by the hair on my chinny chinny chin!

Wolf : Then I'll huff and I'll puff and I'll blow your house down!

Narrator : So the wolf huffed, puffed and blew the house down. The first little pig ran to the house of the second little pig.

Wolf : Little pig, little pig, let me come in!

Pig 2 : Not by the hair on my chinny chinny chin!

Wolf : Then I'll huff and I'll puff and I'll blow your house down.

Narrator : So the wolf huffed, puffed and blew the house down. The two little pigs ran to the house of the third little pig.

Wolf : Little pig, little pig, let me come in!

Pig 3 : Not by the hair on my chinny chinny chin!

Wolf : Then I'll huff and I'll puff and I'll blow your house down.

Narrator : So the wolf huffed and he puffed but he could not blow the house down. The wolf was mad. He jumped up on the roof and slid down the chimney right into a pot of boiling water.

Wolf : Yeow!!!

Narrator : The wolf ran out of the house and the pigs never saw him again!

이상으로 Reading Process에 따른 다양한 활동을 알아봤다. 이제 Balanced Literacy Program의 읽기(reading)에 대해 자세히 알아보자.

3 읽기 구성 요소(Reading Components)

1) 소리 내어 읽기(Modeled Reading 혹은 Read Aloud)

Modeled Reading (혹은 Read Aloud)는 Balanced Literacy Program의 중요한 부분으로 교사는 수업 중에 하루에 몇 번씩 Read Aloud 시간을 가져야 하고, 부모는 적어도 하루에 15분 정도는 아이들에게 책을 읽어 주는 시간을 가져야 한다. Read Aloud는 어린아이들에게 읽기를 가르치는 가장 중요한 첫 단계로, 이 시간을 통해 아이들은 어휘와 이해의 폭이 넓어지고, 동시에 듣기 실력도 향상된다.

(1) 소리 내어 읽기(Modeled Reading 혹은 Read Aloud) 정의

Modeled Reading (혹은 Read Aloud)는 교사가 선택한 글을 학생에게 읽어 주는 것으로, 이 때 선정된 글은 이야기, 시, 신문 기사, 편지글 등 어떤 종류의 글이든지 상관없다. 이 때, 교사는 선택한 글을 학생들에게 유창하게 읽어 주고, 어떻게 글을 이해했는지 그 모습을 직접 보여주게 된다. 이러한 소리 내어 크게 읽어 주는 활동은 초등학교에서 반드시 필요한 읽기활동 중의 하나로, 초보 읽기 학습자가 책을 잘 읽을 수 있게 이끌어 주는데 커다란 영향을 미친다(Trelease 1982). 책을 읽어 주는 것은 초등학교 저학년이나 고학년 어떤 학년에서나 가능하다. 특히 저학년의 경우 학생들이 좋아하는 책을 반복해서 읽어 주는 것도 좋은 방법 중의 하나인데, 되도록 아래에 제시된 자료처럼, 매일매일 다양한 글을 아이들에게 접해 주어 한 장르에 편중되지 않도록 해야 한다.

Monday	Tuesday	Wednesday	Thursday	Friday
Poetry	Letter/Journal	Story	Non-fiction	Class-made text

Read Aloud를 할 때 주의해야 할 사항은 다음과 같다. 아이들이 상상력을 마음껏 펼칠 수 있도록 천천히 읽어 줄 것(read slowly), 교사는 이야기의 내용에 맞게 몸동작을 이용하고, 목소리도 내용에 맞게 감정을 넣어 읽어 줄 것(read with expression), 쉼표와 온점에서는 멈출 것(pause at commas and periods) 등이다. 교사가 즐거운 마음으로 즐기면서 책을 읽어 준다면 그 자체만으로도 교육의 효과는 매우 높다. 아이에게 책을 읽어 줄 때는, 읽어 주는 사람이 실감나고, 재미있게 읽어 주어야 한다. 또한 이야기의 줄거리와 내용을 이해할 수 있도록 여러 가지 질문을 던지는 것이 중요하다. 이 때 아이의 반응을 살펴보면서, 이야기의 결론도 내려보고, 요점도 잡아보고, 스스로 자신의 이야기를 만들어 내어 보게 해야 한다. 이런 과정을 거치면서 아이들은 스스로 책을 읽어 낼 수 있게 되는 것이다. 나중에는 엄마나 교사가 던진 질문을 아이 스스로 만들어 가면서 읽게 만들기 위해서다.

(2) 소리 내어 읽기(Read Aloud)의 효과

아이들에게 Read Aloud를 하면 다음의 효과를 얻을 수 있다.

첫째, 읽기를 배우고자 하는 동기유발을 일으킨다.

둘째, 다양한 비판적 사고를 할 수 있도록 자극을 준다.

셋째, 다양한 장르, 작가, 그림 작가를 알게 된다.

넷째, 책 속에 들어 있는 풍부한 언어를 통해 어휘 량과 글의 이해 폭을 넓힌다.

다섯째, 이야기에 대한 감각(story sense)을 키워준다. 즉, 이야기를 들으면서 이야기의 구조에 익숙해져 이야기의 주인공이 누구인지, 배경은 어디인지, 문제는 무엇이며, 어떻게 해결을 했는지를 이해하고, 결말을 예측하게도 된다.

(3) 소리 내어 읽기(Read Aloud) 수업 절차

실제 Read Aloud 수업을 어떻게 진행해야 하는지 그 순서와 구체적인 방법을 알아보자.

① 수업 계획 세우기 (Plan the Lesson)

- Read Aloud를 할 책 고르기
- 고른 책을 미리 읽어 보기, 읽을 때 초점을 어디에 두고 읽을지 계획세우기 책을 읽어 줄 때에 초점을 맞출 수 있는 소재는 다음과 같다.
  - 주제 (theme) : 책의 주제에 초점을 맞추어 읽기를 한다. 이 때 선택한 주제가 아이들이 소화하기에 어려운 것이라면 주제와 관련된 정보를 미리 준비한다.
  - 작가 (author)/그림 작가(illustrator) : 책을 지은 작가나 그림 작가에 초점을 두고 읽기를 한다. 작가의 다른 작품을 소개하거나, 작가만의 독특한 스타일에 관해 이야기를 나눈다.
  - 장르(genre) : Read Aloud 시간에 중요한 포인트 중의 하나가 여러 장르의 글을 읽어 주는 것이다. 따라서 읽어줄 책이 어떤 장르에 속하는지에 관해 포인트를 둘 수도 있다.

② 책 소개하기 (Introduce the Text)

- 아이들에게 이야기와 관련된 개인적인 경험을 물어본 후에, 책 읽는 즐거움을 더해 줄 수 있는 배경 지식에 관해 이야기를 나눌 수 있다.
- 책의 표지에 관해 이야기하기(Read the cover)

  책의 제목과 작가 그리고 표지의 그림에 관한 이야기를 나눈다.

T : The title is 「*The Rainbow Fish*」. Author and illustrator is Marcus Pfister. He was born in Berne, Switzerland, where he lives today. He is perhaps best known for his series of books featuring Rainbow Fish, which has been published in more than thirty languages around the world.

(책의 제목은 「*The Rainbow Fish*」란다. 글과 그림은 Marcus Pfister가 쓰고 그렸고, 이 사람은 스위스 베르네에서 태어나서 지금도 같은 곳에서 산단다. Marcus Pfister 오늘 읽어 줄 「*The Rainbow Fish*」란 책으로 유명해졌고, 이 책은 전 세계 30개 이상의 언어로 번역되어 출판되었단다.)

• 간략하게 스토리에 관해 설명하기(Explain the story very briefly)

T : The story follows the beautiful Rainbow Fish, who is covered in colorful shiny scales. He thinks that he is better than all the other fish.
(이 책은 반짝이는 비늘로 덮인 아름다운 무지개 물고기에 관한 이야기야. 이 물고기는 자기가 다른 물고기 보다 멋지다고 생각한단다.)

• 이야기 예측하기(Prediction)

그림책을 보여주면서 그림에 관한 이야기를 나눈다. 주인공이 누구를 만났는지, 어디로 가는지, 어떤 문제에 부딪쳤는지, 그 문제를 어떻게 해결해 나가는지 그림을 보면서 페이지마다 이야기를 나누어 본다.

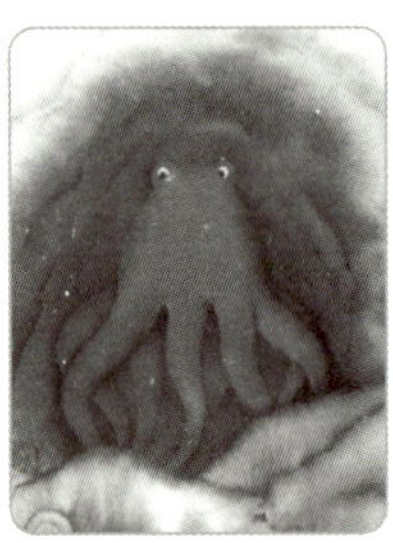

T : The other fish then refuse to talk to the Rainbow Fish at all, so the Rainbow Fish visits the wise female octopus for advice. The octopus advises him to give away his scales to the other fish. Dose the Rainbow Fish gives the small fish his precious scales when he encounters him a second time?
(다른 물고기들이 무지개물고기 이야기하기를 싫어하자, 무지개 물고기는 현명한 문어에게 조언을 청하러 갔지. 문어는 비늘을 나눠 주라고 말했어. 과연 무지개 물고기는 작은 물고기를 다시 만났을 때, 자신의 소중한 비늘을 나누어 주었을까?)

③ 책 소리 내서 읽어 주기(Read the Text Aloud)

• 풍부한 감정을 살려서 책을 읽어 준다.
• 읽어 주는 동안에 중간 중간 너무 많이 쉬거나, 질문을 많이 해서 이야기의 흐름이 끊기지 않도록 한다.

- 읽어 주는 동안에 아이들이 던지는 질문은 자연스럽게 반응한다.
- 읽어 주는 동안 교사는 질문하기(asking questions), 예측하기(making predictions)를 통해서 읽기 전략(reading strategies)을 어떻게 사용하는지 보여 준다.

④ 책으로 다시 돌아가기 (Return to the Text)

- 책을 읽고 난 후에는 아이들에게 책을 읽으면서 느낀 개인의 감정이나 의견을 이야기할 기회를 준다. 「*The Rainbow Fish*」의 경우에는 우정의 중요성에 관한 이야기를 나누고, 물고기 비늘 모양의 종이를 나눠 준 후, 그 종이에 우정에 관한 생각을 적어 보게 한다. 아이들이 적은 비늘을 모아서 큰 무지개 물고기를 만들어 보는 활동을 해 본다.

T : Let's talk about the importance of friendship and make a list on the board of qualities that friends have or should have.
(우정에 관한 이야기를 해 보자. 친구가 가지고 있는 혹은 가져야 하는 것들에는 무엇이 있는지 리스트를 만들어 보자.)
I'll hand out a scale to you. Write a quality that friends have or should have. It could be a sentence or a word. You can decorate your scale if they want.
(선생님이 여러분에게 비늘 모양의 종이를 줄게요. 우정에 필요한 것이 무엇인지 써 보세요. 문장을 써도 좋고, 단어를 써도 되요. 원한다면 비늘을 장식해도 좋아요.)

After you have finished with your scale, put the giant fish on the wall and add your scales to it. You will love seeing the creation of your own giant Rainbow Fish.
(비늘이 모두 완성된 후에는 벽에 커다란 물고기를 붙이고, 거기에 여러분의 비늘을 붙일 겁니다. 여러분이 만든 거대한 무지개물고기를 보면 정말 멋질거에요.)

• 이야기를 요약(summary)하여 말해 보게 한다. 다음은 「*The Rainbow Fish*」 이야기를 요약한 것이다.

There is beautiful fish name Rainbow fish. he thinks he is better than all the other fish and will not play with them. When one small fish asks the Rainbow Fish for one of his scales, he rejects him. Then the other fish refuse to talk to the Rainbow Fish at all, so the Rainbow Fish visits the wise female octopus for advice. The octopus advises him to give away his scales to the other fish. When the Rainbow Fish gives the small fish his precious scales when he encounters him a second time. And he is soon surrounded by other fish requesting scales. Eventually, the Rainbow Fish has only one shiny scale left, but he is no longer vain. He spends his days playing happily with the other fish.

• 빈 칸 채우기 활동(Cloze Activity)을 해 본다. 빈 칸 채우기 활동(Cloze Activity)이란 책의 내용을 요약한 후에 핵심적인 부분의 어휘를 삭제하고 빈칸에 알맞은 단어를 쓰게 하는 활동이다. 다음은 「*The Rainbow Fish*」의 Cloze Activity 문제이다.

▣ Use the following words to fill in the blanks.

The Rainbow Fish is not an _____1_____ fish. He is the most beautiful fish in the _____2_____ ocean. The other fish all _____3_____ his beauty. Once a little blue fish want the Rainbow Fish to give him a shiny ____4____, but the Rainbow Fish didn' t want to. Then the Rainbow Fish become lonely because nobody would play with him anymore. The octopus _____5_____ from the cave, and _____6_____ at the Rainbow Fish. He gave the Rainbow fish some ____7____; that is to share his scales with the other fish, then the octopus _____8____ . The little blue fish followed the Rainbow Fish and ask the Rainbow Fish again to give him a scale. The Rainbow Fish felt _____9_____ giving the little fish the smallest scale, and the little fish swam back and forth showing it off. The others came and ____10____the Rainbow Fish after they saw the little blue fish. So he shared his ____11____scales with them all. After that he was happy as a ____12____.

Answers

1. ordinary	2. entire	3. admired
4. scale	5. emerged	6. glared
7. advice	8. disappeared	9. peculiar
10. surrounded	11. glimmering	12. splash

• 다 읽은 책은 교실에 배치를 해서, 아이들이 책에 쉽게 접근할 수 있게 해야 한다.

(4) 소리 내어 읽기(Read Aloud)하기에 좋은 책

Read Aloud하기에 좋은 책으로는 아이들의 관심과 흥미를 끌 수 있는 것이어야 한다. 그리고 아이들의 상상력을 자극하면서, 구성이 탄탄한 책을 골라야 한다. 특히 우리나라의 경우처럼 영어가 모국어가 아닌 경우에는 Predictable book으로 시작하는 것이 바람직하다.

■ Predictable Book 유형 및 장점

Predictable book이란 라임(rhyme)을 많이 사용해 읽을 때 리듬감이 느껴지고, 단어나 문장이 반복되며, 후렴구가 발달했고, 아이들에게 익숙한 주제를 다룬 책으로, 책을 처음 읽는 아이들도 앞으로 전개될 이야기의 흐름을 예측할 수 있고, 반복이 많은 문장 때문에 읽기가 부담스럽지 않아 기초 단계에서 가장 적합한 책이다. 그렇다면 책의 어떤 요소들이 이런 예측을 가능하게 하는 걸까? Predictable book의 유형을 살펴보자.

Type	Books
Rhyme	• 라임단어(rhyming words)와 후렴구(refrains)가 반복된다. 「*Hop on Pop*」 Seuss, Dr. (1963) 「*Sheep in a Jeep*」 Shaw, Nancy(1988) 「*Jake baked the cake*」 Hennessy, B, G.(1992)
Repetitive Sentences	• 문장이 반복된다. 「*Have you seen my cat?*」 Carle, E. (1991) 「*Good night, gorilla*」 Rathmann, P.(2000) 「*We're going on a bear hunt*」 Rosen, M. (2004)
Sequential Pattern	• 숫자나, 요일처럼 친숙한 패턴으로 책이 구성되어 있다. 「*Today is Monday*」 Carle. E. (1997) 「*10 bears in my bed*」 Makc, S. (1974) 「*Roll over : A counting song*」 Peek, M. (1991)

Pattern Stories	• 새로운 인물이 등장하면서 에피소드가 반복된다. 「*The mitten*」 Brett. J.(1989) 「*Little red hen*」 Galdone. P. (1985) 「*There was an old lady who swallowed fly*」 Taback, S (1997)
Circular Stories	• 이야기의 끝이 다시 시작으로 돌아간다. 「*If you give a mouse a cookie*」 Numeroff, L. J.(1985) 「*The napping house*」 Wood, A.(1984) 「*Why mosquitoes buzz in people's ears*」 Aardema, V. (1992)
Cumulative Stories	• 새로운 에피소드가 소개되면서, 이전의 에피소드가 반복된다. 「*Jack's garden*」 Cole. H. (1997) 「*The old woman and her pig*」 Kimmell, E. A. (1996) 「*This is the house that Jack built*」 Taback, S. (2004)
Questions & Answers	• 질문이 계속 반복된다. 「*Is your mama a lama?*」 Guarino, D. (1989) 「*Where's Spot?*」 Hill, E. (1987) 「*Whose mouse are you?*」 Kraus, R. (1970)
Songs	• 각 페이지에 한 줄 혹은 그 이상의 노래 가사가 반복 된다. 「*Twinkle, twinkle, little star*」 Messenger, J. (1986) 「*Wheels on the bus*」 Raffi. (1988) 「*Down by the bay*」 Raffi.(1999)

이런 Predictable Book의 장점은 다음과 같다.

① 글을 읽지 못하는 아이도 책을 보는 순간부터 자신이 이미 책을 읽고 있다고 생각한다.
(From the very start, children perceive themselves as readers.)

② 아이들은 읽기의 가장 중요한 개념인 '이해'를 하게 된다.
(Children see that reading must make sense.)

③ 아이들은 읽기가 즐거운 활동이라는 것을 알게 된다.
(Children see that reading is an enjoyable activity.)

④ 읽기에서 성취감을 맛본 아이들은 또 읽고 싶어한다
(Children see that books are often read more than once.)

⑤ 교사는 아이들 간의 읽기 차이를 고려해주기 때문에, 읽기가 서투른 아이도 당황하지 않고 다른 아이들로부터 읽기를 배울 수 있다.
(They enable the teacher to provide for individual differences.)

고학년의 경우 위에 제시된 predictable book 수준을 넘어선 책을 읽어 주어야 한다. 다음은 Read-aloud에 좋은 도서 목록이다.

「*Bridge to Terabithia*」 by Katherine Paterson(Harper Collins)
A Newbery Award winner about a boy who becomes a close friend of a new girl in school and suffers agony after her accidental death.

「*Charlotte's Web*」 by E. B. White (Harper Collins)
Classic, whimisical barnyard fable about a spider who saves the life of a pig.

「*Danny, the Champion of the World*」 by Roald Dahl(Econo-Clad Books)
Nine-year-old Danny helps his father on a poaching expedition to wealthy Mr. Hazell's woods.

「*Dear Mr. Henshaw*」 by Beverly Cleary(William Morrow & Co.)
A Newbery Award winner about a boy who pours out his problems in letters to a writer he greatly admires.

「*The Cricket in Times Square*」 by George Selden(Farrar Straus, & Giroux)
A Connecticut cricket is transported in a picnic basket to New York's Times Square

「*Frindle*」 by Andrew Clements(Aladdin)
Nick, a champion time-waster, faces the challenge of his life when confronted with the toughest teacher in the school, Nrs. Granger.

「*From the Mixed - up Files of Mrs. Basil E. Frankweiler*」 by E. L. Konigsburg(Atheneum)
A Newbery Award winner about a 12-year-old girl and her younger brother who eludse security guards and live for a week in New York's Metropolitan Museum of Art.

「*Holes*」 by Louis Sachar(Farrar, Straus, & Giroux)
This Newbery Award winner follows the internment of a boy in a juvenile detention camp who is forced by the warden to dig holes to uncover an outlaw' s hidden treasure.

「*Mrs. Frisby and the Rats of Nimh*」 by Robert O' Brien(Atheneum)
This Newbery Award winner about a group of rats, made literate and given human intelligence, who escape from their laboratory to start their own community.

「*Sarah, Plain and Tall*」 by Patricia MacLachlan(HarperCollins)
A Newbery Award winner about two Children on a prairie who wait for the arrival of their new stepmother.

「*The Secret Garden*」 by Frances Hodgson Burnett(HarperCollins)
Three children find a secret graden and make it bloom again; the garden, in turn, changes the children.

「*Tales of a Fourth Grade Nothing*」 by Judy Blume(E. P. Dutton)
The story of Peter Hatcher's trials and tribulations, most of which are caused by his two-year-old pesky brother, Fudge.

「*How to Eat Fried Worms*」 by Thomas Rockwell(Yearling)
Billy takes on a be-the will eat 15 worms a day. His family and friends help devise ways to cook them.

「*The Hundred Dresses*」 by Eleanor Estes(Harcourt Brace)
A little Polish girl in an American school finally wins acceptance by her classmates.

「*In the Year of the Boar and Jackie Robinson*」 by Bette Bao Lord (HarperCollins)
The story of Chinese girl who leaves China to join her father in New York in 1947.

「*The View from Saturday*」 by E. L. Konigsburg(Atheneum)
A story about a group a of sixth graders chosen to be on the Academic Bowl team.

「*Walk Two Moons*」 by Sharon Creech (HarperCollins)
A Newbery Award winner about a 13-year-old girl journeying to find her mother.

「*James and Giant Peach*」 by Roald Dahl(Knopf)
James is unhappy living with his mean aunts until a magic potion produces an enormous peach, which becomes a home for him.

2) 함께 읽기(Shared Reading)

(1) 함께 읽기(Shared Reading)의 정의

함께 읽기(Shared Reading)는 Holdaway(1979)에 의해 개발된 것으로, 부모나 교사가 아이들과 함께 책을 읽는 것을 뜻한다. 이러한 함께 읽기(Shared Reading)는 영어읽기에 익숙하지 못한 아이들에게 교사나 부모, 혹은 영어 읽기 능력이 뛰어난 친구가 함께 읽으면서 영어 읽기를 도와 주는 방법으로 앞서 살펴본 소리 내어 읽기(Read Aloud)보다는 교사의 역할이 줄어들고, 상대적으로 아이의 역할이 커져서, 함께 읽기(Shared Reading)에서는 아이의 적극적인 읽기 태도가 필요하다. 이 때 책을 잘 고르는 일이 가장 중요한데 예를 들어, 아이가 야구에 관한 지식이 거의 없으면 야구를 소재로 한 책에 흥미를 느끼지 못할 뿐 아니라 그 책을 싫어하게 된다. 따라서 아이의 흥미가 무엇인지 주의 깊게 살펴본 후에 책을 고르는 것이 좋다. 또 부모가 아이와 책을 함께 읽을 책의 크기가 그다지 중요하지 않지만, 학교에서 교사가 많은 아이들과 함께 읽기(Shared Reading)을 할 때는 큰 사이즈의 빅 북(big book)이 필요하다.

(2) 함께 읽기(Shared Reading) 수업 절차

① 수업 계획 세우기(Plan the Lesson)

- 함께 읽기할 책 고르기
  - 읽는 즐거움을 줄 수 있는 책인가?
  - 예상하기 쉬운 이야기(predictable story) 구조인가?

- 새로운 작가인가 아니면 친숙한 작가의 작품인가?
- 한번 이상 다루었던 주제인가 낯선 주제인가?
- 한번 이상 다루었던 장르인가 처음 다루는 장르인가?

위의 질문을 염두에 두고 책을 고른다.

• 아이들을 관찰하면서 교사가 고려해야 할 것
  - 모든 아이들이 읽을 수 있도록 책의 크기나 글씨 크기가 적당한가?
  - 책과 관련되어서 어떤 읽기 기술(Reading Skill)을 가르쳐야 하나?
  - 어떤 읽기 전략(Reading Strategies)을 사용해야 할까?

② 책 소개하기(Introduce the Book/Text)

• 제목, 표지, 작가, 그림 작가에 대해 이야기 나누기
  (Talk about the title, the cover, the author and illustrator)
• 아이들이 가진 배경지식을 나누고, 이야기와 연결지어 보기
  (Share background knowledge and help children make connections)

③ 책 소리 내서 읽어 주기(Read the Book/Text Aloud)

• 읽는 속도가 중요하다.
• 처음 읽어 줄 때는 중간에 멈춤 없이 즐겁게 읽어 준다.
• 아이들의 실제 생활과 이전에 읽었던 스토리와 연결시켜 토론하기

④ 아이들과 함께 책 다시 읽기(Students invited to join in rereading)

• 아이들이 자신감을 갖게 아이들의 참여를 늘린다.
• 작가와 그림 작가의 스타일과 관점을 평가한다.
• 반복되는 패턴과 라임(rhyme)을 확인한다.
• 프린트 컨셉(Print Concept)에 관해 이야기를 나눈다.
• 읽기 전략(Reading Strategies) 시범을 보인다.
• 철자(letters), 단어(words), 문장(sentences), 구두점(punctuation)을 강조한다.
• 파닉스(phonics)를 학습한다.

동시 「*The Little Turtle*」로 실제 수업의 예를 살펴보자.

The Little Turtle

There was a little turtle.
He lived in a box.
He swam in a puddle.
He climbed on the rocks.
He snapped at a mosquito.
He snapped at a flea.
He snapped at a minnow.
And he snapped at me.
He caught the mosquito.
He caught the flea.
He caught the minnow.
But he didn't catch me

Shared reading 시간을 통해서 철자(letters)와 소리(sound), 철자 패턴(spelling patterns)과 단어(words)를 배우게 된다.

T : Let's look at our poem about the turtle. Let's reread these four lines.
(The turtle이란 시를 봅시다. 네 번째 줄을 다시 읽어 볼까요?)

S : He snapped at a mosquito. He snapped at a flea. He snapped at a minnow. And he snapped at me.
(그는 모기를 잡아챘다. 그는 벼룩을 잡아챘다. 그는 작은 물고기를 잡아챘다. 그리고 그는 나를 잡아챘다.)

T : (Points to the words mosquito and minnow as she says them) What is it about these two words that is the same?
('mosquito' and 'minnow'를 말하면서 두 단어를 지적한다.)(이 두 단어에서 무엇이 같은가요?)

S : They start the same.
(같은 철자로 시작해요.)

T : Good checking! Yes, they do begin with the same sound. These two words start with the letter m, just like one of the pictures on our alphabet chart. Who can find it?
(좋은 지적이에요. 그래요. 두 단어는 같은 소리로 시작해요. 이 두 단어는 철자 m으로 시작해요. 알파벳 차트에서 m으로 시작하는 그림은 무엇이 있나요?)

S : I can! Magnet!
(저요, magnet이요.)

T : Yes! Mosquito and minnow do start like magnet on the alphabet chart. Go and point to that letter on the alphabet chart while we read it.
(네, Mosquito, minnow은 magnet처럼 m으로 시작해요. 우리가 읽는 동안에 알파벳차트에서 해당 철자를 지적하세요.)

S : (Chanting) M, m, magnet!
(M, m, magnet!)

T : Mosquito, minnow, and magnet all begin the same. Are there any other words in our poem that start like mosquito, minnow, and magnet?
(Mosquito, minnow, magnet은 모두 같은 소리로 시작해요. Mosquito, minnow, magnet처럼 같은 소리로 시작하는 단어를 시에서 찾을 수 있나요?)

S : Me does!
(Me 요.)

T : That's super! Me does begin with the same sound and letter as mosquito, minnow, and magnet.
(잘했어요. Me란 단어도 Mosquito, minnow, magnet처럼 모두 같은 소리와 철자로 시작해요.)

■ 프린트 컨셉(Print Concept)

– Print Concept이란 문자언어(written language)에 대해 명확하게 개념을 잡은 것으로, 다음에 제시된 체크리스트를 참고하기 바란다.

Concepts of Print Individual Checklist

Student :________________ Grade :________________

Teacher Questions	√	Concepts
Before reading, ask the child: Show me the front of the book.		front cover
Show me the back of the book.		back cover
Point to the title.		convention
Point to the title page.		convention
Which page do we read first?		directionality
Where does it tell the story?		print carries the message.
Which way do we go when we' re reading?		directionality
Where do we go when we get to the end of the line?		directionality and return sweep
During reading ask yourself: As the child read and points to the text, is there an exact match between number of words spoken and the number of words printed?		Concept of a word, one-to-one correspondence
After reading, ask the child: Can you find two words that are the same?		Concept of a word
Show me the first word on this page.		Concept of beginning, middle and end
Show me the last word on this page.		Concept of beginning, middle and end

Can you find a capital letter?		capital letter
Can you find a small letter?		lower case letter
What does this mean when I am reading. Point to: "." (period)		punctuation
"," (coma)		punctuation
"?" (question mark)		punctuation
"!" (exclamation mark)		punctuation
" " (quotation marks)		punctuation

Print concept의 실제 수업 예를 보자.

T : I'm going to read you this story but I want you to help me.

Test : For orientation of book.

T : (Pass the book to the child.) Show me the front of this book.

Test : Concept that print carries the message.

T : I'll read this story. You help me. Show me where to start reading. Where do I begin to read?

Test : For the direction rules.

T : Show me where to start.

Test : Moves left to right on any line.

T : Which way do I go?

Test : Return sweep.

T : Where do I go after that?

Test : Word-by-word pointing.

T : Point to it while I read it.

Test : Concept of first and last.

T : Show me the first part of the story. Show me the last part.

Test : A left page is read before a right page.
T : Where do I start reading?

Test : Punctuation
T : What's this for?

Test : Capital and lower case letters.
T : Find a little letter like this.

Test : Word concept.
T : Show me just one word. Now show me two words.

Test : First and last letter concepts.
T : Show me the first letter of a word.
T : Show me the last letter of a word.

▣ 읽기전략(Reading Strategies)

흔히 Reading은 작가와 독자 사이의 대화라고 한다. 그 대화를 제대로 하기 위해서는 독자는 특별한 행동을 취해야 하는데, 그런 행동을 일컬어 Reading Strategies라고 한다. 이 Reading Strategies는 크게 둘로 나눌 수 있는데, 하나는 단어인지(word recognition)를 위한 전략과, 다른 하나는 이해(reading comprehension)를 위한 전략이다.

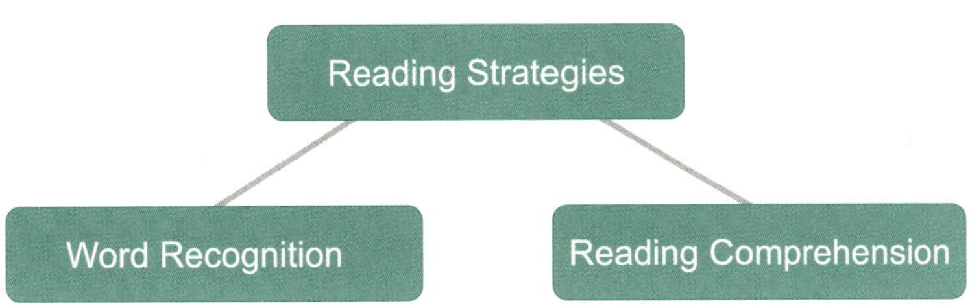

단어인지(word recognition)를 할 때 사용할 수 있는 읽기 전략으로는 Three Cueing System이 있다. Three Cueing System 이란 말 그대로 책을 읽을 때 세 가지 단서(cue)를 이용하는 것으로, 다음의 그림을 참고로 해서 보다 구체적인 내용을 살펴보자.

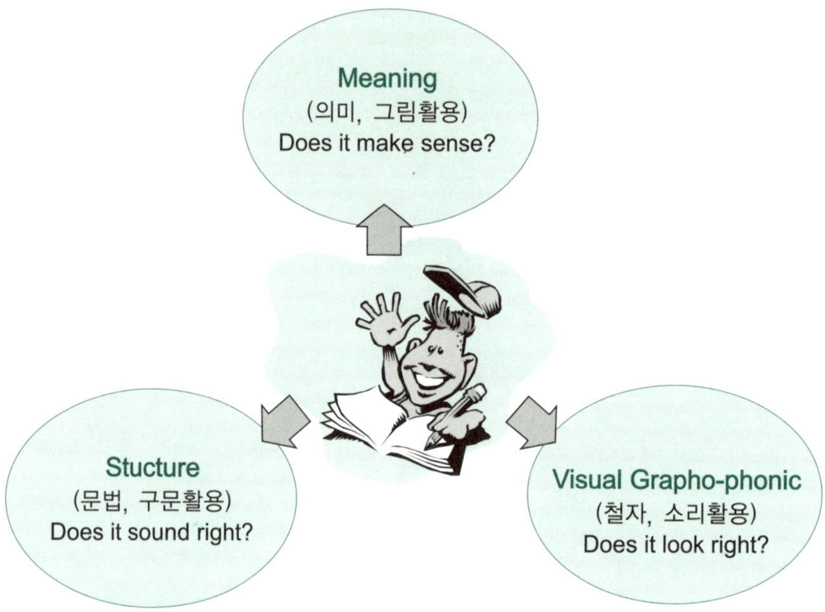

※ Meaning 활용 방법(의미나 그림을 활용)

"Does it make sense?"(말이 되나?/뜻이 통하나?)란 질문을 하며 읽어내는 것이다.

예 책에 제시된 문장 : *The **house** had four bedrooms.*

아이가 읽은 문장 : *The **horse** had four bedrooms.*

T : Does that make sense? Does a horse have bedrooms? The word starts like horse. What would make sense? Can you guess what has bedrooms?
(지금 읽은 문장이 말이 되니? 말이 침실이 있나요? 말과 비슷한 단어로 시작하는구나. 어떤 단어를 넣으면 의미가 통할까? 침실이 있는 것은 어디인지 추측할 수 있겠니?)

책에 제시된 house란 단어를 horse라고 읽은 경우, 이 두 단어는 아이의 눈에는 매우 흡사해 보이며, 문장구조상으로도 문제가 없다. 그러나 의미(meaning)면에서는 맞지가 않기 때문에 교사는 즉각 질문을 던져 아이의 오류를 수정해 주어야 한다.

※ Structure 활용방법(문법이나 구문을 활용)

예 책에 제시된 문장 : *The goat* ***ate*** *four shoes.*
아이가 읽은 문장 : *The goat* ***eated*** *four shoes.*

T : Do you say, 'the goat eated'? Does that sound right? What sound would be better?
(the goat eated라고 읽었지요? 그렇게 읽는 것이 옳으니? 어떻게 소리를 내야 옳을까요?)

※ Visual/Grapho – Phonic의 활용방법(철자와 소리를 활용)

철자와 소리를 맞춰가며 단어를 읽는 것으로, 단어의 처음, 가운데, 마지막 철자에 유의하며 발음해 본다. "Does it look right?"(옳은 것 같니?)란 질문을 하며 읽어낸다.

예 책에 제시된 문장 : *He jumped over the* ***gate.***
아이가 읽은 문장 : *He jumped over the* ***fence.***

T : That was a good try. He jumped over the fence, but does the word look like fence? What would you expect to see at the beginning of the word 'fence'? Is this an 'f'? (Teacher points to the letter 'g'.) What sound does 'g' make?
(잘 읽었구나. *He jumped over the fence.*라고 읽었는데, 이 글자가 fence로 보이니? fence란 단어의 첫 자는 어떻게 발음이 되지? 그래, 그럼 이 글자가 f니? ('g'를 가리키면서) 그러면 'g'는 무슨 소리를 낼까?)

초급 단계의 독자는 책을 읽다가 모르는 단어가 나올 때는 읽기 전략으로 Three cueing system을 사용하게 된다. 또 다른 읽기 전략은 이해(comprehension)로 아이들은 스스로 질문을 만들고(ask questions), 시각화하고(visualize), 정보를 종합하고(synthesize information), 추론해서(make inferences) 책의 핵심 내용을 파악하게 된다. 다음은 아이들이 읽기 전략을 제대로 쓰고 있는지 알아볼 수 있는 체크리스트이다.

Reading Strategies Checklist

Student:__________________ Grade :______________________

Before Reading

_____I think about the cover, title, and what I know about the topic.

_____I skim, looking at and thinking about illustrations, photos, graphs, and charts.

_____I read headings and captions.

_____I read the back cover and/or print inside of the jacket or the source (journals and magazines or Internet source).

_____I ask questions. These may be written or in my head.

_____I make predictions about the material I am about to read. These may be written or in my head.

During Reading

_____I make mental pictures. I can visualize what I am reading about.

_____I identify confusing parts and reread them. I make notes for assistance.

_____I use pictures, graphs, and charts to understand confusing parts.

_____I identify unfamiliar words and use context clues to figure out their meanings or write them down and look up their meaning.

_____I stop and retell to see what I remember. If necessary, I reread.

_____I predict and adjust or confirm.

_____I raise questions and read on to discover answers.

_____I jot down a tough word and the page it's on and ask for help.

After Reading

_____I think about the characters, setting, events, of new information.

_____I identify the theme or thesis (main idea) of what I have read.

_____I discuss or write my reactions. Do I agree or disagree?

_____I reread parts I enjoy or that seem to be meaningful to me.

_____I re-skim to find details.

_____I reread to find support for questions.

_____I can summarize what I have read.

⑤ 책 읽고 반응하기(Respond to the Text)

- 이야기 지도를 만든다.(Story mapping)
- 작가에 대해 연구한다.(Author study)
- 연극을 한다.(Acting out story)
- 토론을 한다.(Discussion)
- 리텔링을 한다.(Retelling)
- 학생들이 함께 빅북을 만든다.(Class-made Big Book)
- 만들기를 한다.(Arts and crafts)

▣ 이야기 지도(Story Map)

Story Map이란 이야기이 해신요소 인 등장인물(characters), 상소(place), 시간(time), 사건(event) 등을 지도처럼 도식화하여 나타내는 것을 말한다.

「Have you ever seen my cat?」

한 소년이 잃어버린 고양이를 찾아 나선다. 소년이 만나는 사람들은 여러 나라의 사람들이다. 그들이 가르쳐 주는 곳으로 가 보면 사자, 삵괭이, 표범, 퓨마, 치타 등 고양이과의 동물들을 만나게 된다. 소년은 공원 저 편에서 단란한 가족을 이루고 있는 자신의 고양이를 찾게 된다.

Story Map

Have you ever seen my cat?
By Eric Carle

▼

Character : Little boy | Places: Different places

▼

Problem : The boy lost the cat. He asks many people for knowledge of his cat.

▼

Solution : The boy finally finds his cat.

▣ 작가 연구(Author Study)

아이들이 책을 읽다보면 자연스럽게 좋아하는 작가가 생기게 된다. 이 작가들에 대해 자료를 수집해서 다음과 같은 파일을 만들어 보자. 작가 홈페이지에 가보면 사진이외의 많은 정보를 얻을 수 있다.

Name	Photo here
Country of Origin :	Education History

Date of Birth : Life History :
Book Written
My favorite book by this author is : Because :

(3) 함께 읽기(Shared Reading)하기에 좋은 책

함께 읽기(Shared Reading)하기에 좋은 책은 아이들의 관심과 흥미를 끌 수 있는 책으로 단어나 문장이 후렴구처럼 반복이 되어 아이들이 글자를 모르더라도 유추하여 읽어낼 수 있는 것이 좋다. 이 과정을 통해 아이들이 스스로 읽어 냈다는 자신감을 얻게 된다. 또한 책의 문장은 간결하고 짧은 게 좋은데, 책의 문장이 너무 길거나 복잡하면, 아이들이 따라 읽는 데 어려움을 겪기 때문이다. 따라서 앞서 설명한 predictable book이나 라임(rhyme: hat과 cat처럼 끝소리가 같은 단어)이 많은 마더구스(mothergoose)와 같이 아이들이 책을 읽을 때 리듬을 타서 유창하게 읽을 수 있는 책이 좋다.

▣ 마더구즈(Mothergoose)

(「다중지능을 활용한 유이영이교육」, 임정현 · 오현수, 2006에서 발췌)

세계 여러 나라에는 민족 특유의 정서가 녹아있는 전래동요가 있다. 이러한 전래동요를 프랑스에서는 비에일 샹송(vielles chansons)이라고 하고, 독일에서는 포크스리더(vokslieder)라고 하며, 미국을 포함한 영미 문화권에서는 마더구즈(mothergoose)라고 한다. 즉 마더구즈란 오랜 옛날부터 구전되어 내려오는 영어권 아이들의 노래를 총칭해서 부르는 말로, '마더구즈' 라는 여인(큰 거위를 타고 다녀서 마더구즈라고 이름이 붙음) 전래동요를 수집, 정리했다고 전해지고 있다. 이러한 마더구즈의 중요성을 정리하면 다음과 같다.

첫째, 아이가 접하는 최초의 문학이다. 마더구즈는 그 자체가 하나의 이야기이자 가장 압축된 형태의 문학구조를 가지고 있다. 문학구조를 가지고 있다는 것은 이야기 속에 인물(character), 사건(plot), 배경(setting)이 있다는 것으로, 차후에 긴 형태의 문학작품을 접하더라도 그 의미를 쉽게 파악할 수 있다. 마더구즈 'Jack and Jill' 의 경우를 살펴보자.

Jack and Jill

Jack and Jill went up the hill
To fetch a pail of water
Jack fell down and broke his crown
And Jill came tumbling after.

마더구즈를 통해서 다음의 질문에 답할 수 있다.

Who are the main characters?(주인공은 누구인가요?)

What did the story take place?(이야기가 일어난 장소는 어딘가요?)

What happen to them?(무슨 일이 일어났나요?)

둘째, 영미권 문화에 대해 이해를 할 수 있다. 깊이 있는 영어를 구사하기 위해서는 영미 문화에 관해서도 알아야 하는데, 영미 문화가 그대로 녹아있는 것이 바로 마더구즈다. 잘 알려진 마더구즈 'London Bridge' 의 노래 속에 담긴 역사를 알아보자.

London Bridge

London Bridge is falling down, falling down, falling down.
London Bridge is falling down, my fair lady.
Built it up with iron bars, iron bars, iron bars.
Built it up with iron bars, my fair lady.
Iron bars will bend and break, bend and break, bend and break.
Iron bars will bend and break, my fair lady.
Built it up with silver and gold, silver and gold, silver and gold,
Built it up with silver and gold, my fair lady.

이 노래 속에 담긴 역사를 살펴보면 가사에서도 나와 있듯이, 실제 'London Bridge'가 여러 번 무너졌었고, 이 다리가 튼튼하고 오래가길 빌면서 다리 아래에다 살아있는 사람을 생매장하거나 강물에 던지는 풍습이 있었다고 한다. 그래서 이 노래를 부를 때는 흔히 하는 놀이로 아치게임(arch game)을 하는데, 두 명이 손을 마주잡아 아주 높이 올려 다리모양을 만들면, 다른 아이들이 줄을 지어 그 밑으로 지나가다가 한 명을 붙잡는 놀이이다. 이처럼 마더구즈를 통해서 자연스럽게 영미문화와 역사도 익힐 수 있다.

셋째, 마더구즈는 다양한 형태의 영어 학습에 사용될 수 있다. 'Humpty Dumpty' 로 그 예를 살펴보자.

Humpty Dumpty

Humpty Dumpty sat on the wall,
Humpty Dumpty had a great fall.
All the king's horses
And all the king's men
Couldn't put Humpty Dumpty
Together again.

'Humpty Dumpty' 를 배우면서 알파벳 'H, h' 의 모양과 소리를 읽히고, 'wall, fall' 처럼 끝이 같은 소리로 끝나는 'rhyming words' 도 배울 수 있다.

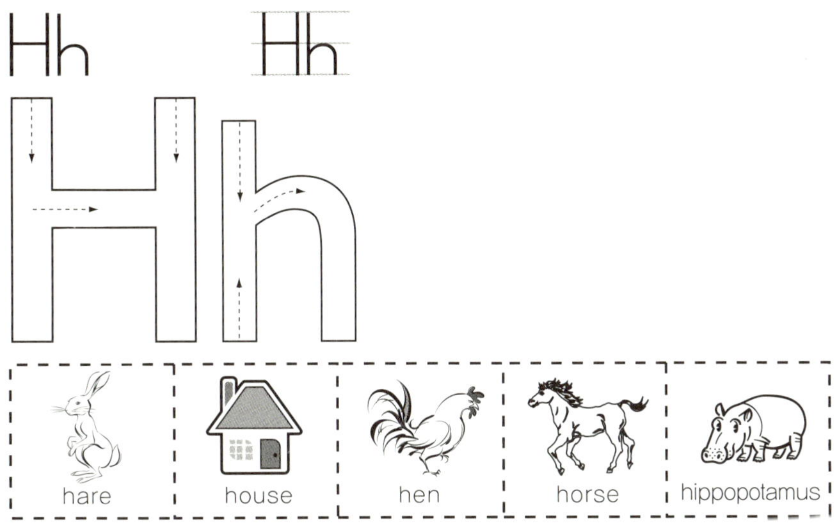

(자료출처 : http://www.first-school.ws/t/alpha1/h.htm)

[Teacher's Talk]

What letter is this?(이 글자의 이름은 무엇인가요?)
What sound is this?(어떤 소리가 날까요?)
Tell me three words begins with h.(철자 h로 시작하는 세 단어를 말하세요.)
Trace the letter h.(철자 h를 따라 써 보세요.)

Rhyming Words

[Teacher's Talk]

Find the words.(단어를 찾아보세요)
It begins with /b/and ends with the rhyme /-all/.(/b/로 시작하고 /all/로 끝나요.)
Let's put them together. What word is it?(둘을 합치면 어떤 단어가 되나요?)

3) 유도된 읽기(Guided Reading)

(1) 유도된 읽기(Guided Reading)의 정의

유도된 읽기(Guided Reading)는 읽기 수준이 비슷한 4~6명 정도의 소그룹을 구성한 후 아이들 모두에게 같은 책을 나눠 준다. 이 때, 글의 수준은 아이들이 읽기에 충분히 쉽고, 문제해결을 위한 도전의 기회를 주되, 유창하게 읽는 데에 방해되지 않는 수준이어야 한다. 또, 교사의 티칭 포인트는 책을 읽는 과정에서 모르는 단어가 나오는 경우, 전후의 내용을 유추하고 자신만의 읽기 전략(reading strategies)을 동원하여 단어의 의미를 파악하게 하는 문제해결 능력을 키우는 것에 초점을 맞춰야 한다. 이러한 과정을 거쳐 아이들은 자연스럽게 읽기 전략(reading strategies)을 마스터하게 되고, 차후 아이들이 혼자서 읽을 수 있는 단계 (Independent Reading)로 나아가게 된다. 유도된 읽기(Guided Reading)는 보통 초등 저학년 과정에서 많이 적용되고 있지만, 우리나라와 같은 비영어권 환경에서는 초등 고학년에게도 매우 효과적인 읽기 지도 방법이다.

(2) 유도된 읽기(Guided Reading) 수업 절차

① 수업 계획 세우기(Plan the Lesson)

- 유도된 읽기(Guided Reading)할 책 고르기
  - 교사는 아이들의 읽기 수준에 따라 그룹을 나누고, 각 그룹마다 수업의 초점을 어디에다 둘지 결정한 후, 그룹의 수준에 적정한 책을 고른다.
  - 교사는 책을 어떻게 소개할지, 어떤 읽기전략(reading strategies)을 보여줄지 계획을 세운다.

② 책 소개하기(Introduce the Book/Text)

- 교사는 책을 소개할 때, 다음에 제시한 요소 중 몇 가지를 선택하여 아이들과 이야기를 나눈다.
  - 그림에 대해 이야기 나누기(Talk about the illustrations)
  - 이야기의 기본 구성에 대해 이야기 나누기(Talk basic plot)
  - 아이들에게 예측하게 하게 한다.(Have students make predictions)
  - 읽기 전략에 관해 도론한나.(Discuss reading strategies)
  - 어려운 단어나 구문에 대해 살펴본다.(Anticipate challenging words and structure)

③ 아이들이 책읽기/개인별 피드백하기(Read the text/Provide Individual Feedback)

- 교사가 아이들이 읽는 것을 체크하기 위해 돌아다니는 동안, 아이들은 스스로 책을 읽는다.
- 교사는 개별적으로 아이가 읽는 것을 듣고, 관찰 한 후 필요할 경우 개별 코치를 한다.

④ 책으로 다시 돌아가기(Return to the Text)

- 토론하기(Discussion) : 아이들이 이해한 것을 명확하게 하기 위해 같이 토론을 한다.

• 학습 포인트(Teaching points) : 아이들이 읽기를 하는 동안에 관찰했던 것을 기초로 해서 학습 포인트를 한두 개 골라서 강조한다. 이 때의 포인트는 파닉스나 단어, 읽기 전략 등이 될 수 있다.

⑤ 수업평가하기(Assess the Lesson)

• 교사는 아이들 하나하나를 관찰한 결과를 기록하고, 아이들에게 무엇을 더 가르쳐야 하는지 결정을 한다. 이 결과는 다음 수업 계획에 즉시 반영한다.

다음은 미국 1학년 아이들과 교사가 Guided Reading하는 모습을 정리한 것이다. 교사가 선정한 책은 「*The Lion's Tale*(Scott Foresman)」으로 꼬리를 찾을 수 없어서 슬퍼하는 사자의 이야기이다. (「*Guided Reading: Making It Works*」, Scholastic. 발췌)

T : 「*The Lion's Tail*」 is a story about a lion who is very sad because he can't find his tail. Some animal friends come along and ask him why he's sad. This story begins like make-believe stories. Do you know some of the ways make-believe stories can begin?
(「*The Lion's Tail*」은 꼬리를 못 찾아서 슬퍼하는 사자 이야기죠. 다른 동물 친구들이 사자에게 왜 슬픈지 물어봅니다. 이 이야기는 만들어진 이야기(make-believe)로 시작하네요. 만들어진 이야기(make-believe)가 어떤 식으로 시작하는지 아나요?)

S1 : Once upon a time?
(옛날에?)

S2 : A long ago.
(예전에)

T : You're both right. Take a look at the first page to see how this story begins. Let's read it together.
(둘 다 맞아요. 이야기가 어떻게 시작하는지 첫 페이지를 봅시다.)
(The students and a teacher read the first sentence, "Once upon a time a lion couldn't find his tail.")

T : There's a word I want you to look at in the sentence "Once upon a time a lion couldn't find his tail." It's on other pages in the book too. It's the word couldn't. Can you find it?
("Once upon a time a lion couldn't find his tail." 문장에서 여러분이 봐야할 단어가 있어요. 다른 페이지에서도 나오는데, 그 단어는 couldn't에요. 여러분이 찾을 수 있나요?)
(Students locate couldn't.)

T : It's another way of saying could not. We'll talk more about words like couldn't after you read. We know the lion's sad because he couldn't find his tail. Look at the picture. Who came along to help him?
(다른 표현으로는 could not이 있어요. 다 읽고 난 다음에 couldn't 와 같은 단어에 대해 이야기해봅시다. 사자가 꼬리를 찾지 못해서 슬프다는 건 다 알고 있지요. 누가 사자를 도와 주나요?)

S 1 : A mouse.
(생쥐요.)

T : The mouse wants to know why the lion's so sad. Let's turn the page and see what the lion says.
(생쥐는 사자가 왜 슬픈지 알고 싶어요. 다음 페이지를 넘겨서, 사자가 뭐라고 하는지 봅시다.)

(Students look at pages 4 & 5.)

T : He said, "I…"
(그는 말하길 "I…")
(Students say : can't find my tail.")

T : So the mouse helped him look for it. But you know what? He couldn't find the lion's tail. Look through the rest of the book to see who else helped and who found his tail.
(그래서 생쥐는 꼬리 찾는 것을 도와줍니다. 그런데, 생쥐는 사자의 꼬리를 찾을 수 없었어요. 누가 사자를 도와주고, 누가 사자의 꼬리를 찾는지 책의 나머지 부분을 살펴 봅시다.)
(Students continue to look through the book on their own and make comments about other animal characters and events.)

T : So where was the lion's tail?
(그래서 사자의 꼬리는 어디에 있었나요?)

S : He was sitting on it.
(사자가 깔고 앉아 있었어요.)

T : How do you know?
(어떻게 알았나요?)

S : I looked at the picture.
(그림을 보고 알았어요.)

T : The pictures can help, can't they?
(그림은 이해하는데 도움을 줘요.)

T : Now you're ready to read the story on your own. Remember to think about the story and what's happening as you read.
(이제, 여러분 스스로 이야기를 읽을 준비가 되었어요. 읽는 동안에 어떤 일이 벌어지고 있는지 이야기에 관해서 기억을 하기 바랍니다.)

Students read softly to themselves at the table while a teacher observes their reading. She notices that Lucas is reading word by word and decided to show how to read groups of words to make his reading more phrased and fluent.
(학생들은 조용하게 책을 읽고, 교사는 읽는 것을 관찰한다. 그러다가 Lucas가 단어를 하나씩 읽는 것을 보면서 더 유창하게 읽기 위해서는 단어를 어떻게 묶음으로 읽는지 알려준다.)

T : Listen to how I read this. I'm going to read it like the character is talking, "/I can't/… find may tail./" You try it.
(선생님이 읽는 걸 들어보세요. 나는 등장인물이 말하는 것처럼 읽을 겁니다. "/I can't/ …find may tail./" 해보세요.)
(Lucas echoes the phrasing of the sentence.)

T : Here's how I would read this part. /I'll /…look for it./ You try.
(선생님이 여기 이 부분을 읽을게요. /I'll /…look for it./ 해보세요.)
(Lucas repeats the sentence.)

T : Now when you come to the parts where characters talk, make it sound like they're talking by reading groups of words.
(이제, 등장인물이 이야기하는 부분이 나오면, 단어를 묶음으로 읽어서 마치 그들이 이야기하는 것처럼 소리 내어 보세요.)

(Teacher continues to listen to Lucas read and acknowledges once or twice when he reads groups of words in a phrased and fluent manner.)
(교사는 Lucas가 읽는 것을 계속 들으면서, 단어를 묶음으로 읽고 유창하게 읽는 것을 인정한다.)

(3) 유도된 읽기(Guided Reading)하기에 좋은 책

Guided Reading 과정에서는 도서의 선정이 무엇보다 중요한데, 다음의 제시되는 내용을 참고해서 아이에게 맞은 책을 골라야 한다.

- 아이들의 언어 수준에 맞아야 한다.(읽기 정확도 90% 이상)
- 아이들의 지식(인지)수준에 맞아야 한다.
- 아이들이 흥미를 느끼는 책이어야 한다.

이러한 책을 고르기가 어려울 경우는 이미 책의 수준이 정해져서 나오는 Leveled Books(Leveled Readers)를 선택하여 읽히는 것도 좋다.

▣ 단계별 리더스(Leveled Readers)

아동 문학의 범주에 속하는 Authentic Story Book, 즉 창작 그림책과는 별도로 아이들이 읽기를 시작할 때 쉽게 접해줄 수 있는 책이 바로 Leveled Readers다. 이 책은 작품성이나 문학성보다는 언어의 습득이나 파닉스 개념의 이해처럼 학습적인 것에 그 목표를 두고 있고, 그에 따라 단계별이나 연령별로 난이도를 두어서 등급을 나누고 있다. 많은 출판사들이 각 출판사마다 다양한 종류의 책이 등급별로 출간하고 있으며, 시리즈에 따라서는 수십, 수백 종이 있기도 하다.

다음은 대표적인 Leveled Books들이다.

4) 독립된 읽기(Independent Reading)

(1) 독립된 읽기(Independent Reading)의 정의

독립된 읽기(Independent Reading)는 아이들 스스로 책을 선택한 후, 지금까지 배운 읽기 전략(reading strategies)을 직접 적용시켜서 읽기를 하는 시간으로 책읽기의 즐거움을 경험하게 된다.

이와 같은 독립된 읽기(Independent Reading)를 격려하기 위해서는 그 의미를 정확히 이해해야 하는데, 독립된 읽기(Independent Reading)란 함께 읽기(Shared Reading)도 아니고, 유도된 읽기(Guided Reading)도 아니다. 즉 아이가 책을 읽고 있을 때, 부모나 교사는 아이의 책읽기에 개입을 하지 않아야 한다는 것이다.

또 독립된 읽기(Independent Reading)에서의 중요한 핵심은 아이 스스로 책을 골라야 한다는 것이다. 아이가 책의 글을 모두 읽을 수 없어도 상관없다. 예를 들어 세 살된 아이가 책꽂이에서 그림책을 꺼내서 혼자 읽는다고 생각해 보자. 이것이 독립된 읽기(Independent Reading)의 시작인 것이다. 이 시간을 통해서 아이는 상상력과, 이해력, 단어 인지력, 유창성, 어휘력의 향상될 뿐만 아니라, 주제에 관한 흥미를 키울 수 있게 된다.

한 가지 명심해야 할 것은 독립된 읽기(Independent Reading)가 어느 날 갑자기 나타나는 현상이 아니란 것이다. 따라서 부모와 교사는 책읽기가 습관이 될 수 있도록 적극적인 역할을 해야 한다.

아이가 독립된 읽기(Independent Reading)에 흥미를 가질 수 있게 할 수 있는 가장 좋은 방법은 부모나 교사 스스로 독립된 읽기(Independent Reading)가 되는 것이다. TV를 끄고, 책을 펼쳐 봐야 한다.

하루가 끝나는 무렵에는 가족들이 둘러 앉아 음악을 들으면서 자유롭게 읽기 시간을 가지는 것도 좋은 방법이다. 아이는 놀라운 흉내쟁이이기 때문에, 부모나 교사가 책읽기를 좋아하면 할수록, 아이 역시 책읽기를 자연스럽게 여기게 된다. 교사의 경우 일정한 시간을 정해서 아이들이 책읽기를 할 수 있도록 하는 것이 좋다.

(2) 독립된 읽기(Independent Reading) 수업 모습

다음은 independent reading 수업을 하는 모습을 정리한 것이다.

위에 제시한 내용에서 볼 수 있는 읽기 방법을 수평선 읽기(horizontal reading)라고 하는데, 수평선 읽기란 같은 수준의 책을 여러 권 읽는 것으로, 이 과정을 통해서 어휘의 수준이 서서히 늘면서 그 결과 읽기의 수준 높아지게 된다.

Teacher explains to the class that she is going to set the timer for five minutes, and during these five minutes, everyone has to be looking at a book. When Independent Reading time is over, children are encouraged to put their books back carefully in the same container or place from which they selected the book. Covers should be facing out and books should be placed right side up.
(교사는 타이머를 5분에 맞춰 놓고, 이 5분간 모든 아이들이 책을 볼 거라고 설명한다. Independent Reading 시간이 끝나고, 아이들은 책을 제 자리에 가져다 놓는다. 표지가 보이도록 책을 바르게 꽂아 놓아야 한다.)

After it is over, teacher pulls aside the children who had an especially difficult time sitting with a book for five whole minutes. They discuss again how they can look at the pictures to try to figure out what the story is about or to name the colors they see on the pages, or how they can go through and think of the names of as many things as possible pictured on each page.

(수업이 끝나고, 교사는 5분의 시간동안 책읽기를 어려워한 아이들의 옆에 다가간다. 그리고 이야기를 이해하기 위해서 어떻게 그림을 봐야하는지, 아이들이 봤던 색의 이름도 말해 보고, 각 페이지에 있는 그림의 이름을 말해보기도 한다.)

Teacher has to do this several times, but by the end of the month the children really can sit still with a book for five minutes. Teacher will extend the reading time to ten minutes and will hold that level for a while.
(교사가 이런 활동을 몇 차례 반복 하고나면, 그 달이 끝날 무렵 아이들은 5분 동안 조용히 앉아서 책을 읽을 수 있게 된다. 교사는 책을 읽는 시간을 10분을 늘이고, 당분간 같은 레벨의 책을 읽도록 지도한다.)

(3) 어떤 책을 선택해서 읽을 것인가?

아이가 혼자 읽기 수준에 도달했다고 해서 아이를 그냥 내버려 두어서는 안 된다. 이것은 마치 소에게 혼자 밭을 갈라고 하고 주인은 없어지는 것과 같은 것이다. 이 시기에도 교사와 부모는 학생을 도와 주고 격려해 주어야 한다. 특히 가장 중요한 역할은 책 선정에 도움을 주어야 한다. 아이가 혼자 읽을 수 있다고 해서 아무 책이나 골라 읽다가는 자칫 책읽기에 문제가 발생할 수 있기 때문이다. 아이에게 너무 쉽지도, 너무 어렵지도 않은 아이의 의 수준에 딱 맞는 책을 골라야 하는데, 그런 책을 고르려면 어떻게 해야 할까?

▣ 다섯 손가락 규칙(The Five Finger Rule)

만약 아이가 고른 책이 아이에게 딱 맞는 이른바 "just right" 책인지 아닌지를 알 수 있는 방법으로는 다섯 손가락 규칙(The Five Finger Rule)이 있다. 이 방법은 책의 첫 페이지를 편 다음, 읽기 시작해서 모르는 단어가 나올 때마다 손가락으로 개수를 센다. 한 페이지를 다 읽은 후에, 몇 개의 손가락이 접혔는지 체크를 한다. 이 때 모르는 단어가 0~1개이면 그 책은 너무 쉽고(too easy), 모르는 단어가 4~5개 이상이면 그 책은 아이의 수준에 비해 너무 어려운 책이고, 모르는 단어가 2~3개 정도 되면 바로 그 책이 아이의 수준에 딱 맞는("just right") 책이 되는 것이다. 이렇게 딱 맞는 책을 고른 후에는 앞서 설명한 읽기전략(Reading Strategies)을 적용시켜서 책을 읽는데, 초보자의 경우에는 글자를 해독하는 전략(decoding strategies)을 사용해야 한다.

이 해독전략은 먼저 글을 소리 내서 읽도록 입을 준비시킨 후(get your mouth ready), 그림을 보고(look at the picture), 단어를 소리 내서 읽어 보게(say all the sounds)한다. 이 때 항상 앞서 말한 세 가지 단서(three cueing system)의 질문 'Does it look right?, Does it sound right?, Does it make sense?' 를 하면서 책을 읽어야 한다. 이렇게 자신의 읽기 수준에 맞는 책을 읽어 가다보면 차후에 읽기 수준은 점점 높아지게 된다. 다음은 영미권 아동 문학상에 대해 정리해 보고, 어떤 작품들이 있는지 알아보자.

▣ 영미권 아동문학상

2007년 미국에서만 출간된 어린이 서적이 26,000여 권이라고 한다. 그 중에서 아동문학상에 선정되는 도서는 미국과 영국의 모든 도서관에 비치될 뿐만 아니라 전 세계로 번역, 출간되어 아이들의 필독서로 널리 읽혀지게 된다. 또 명작으로 평가받아 교과서에 실리는 경우도 많다. 아이들에게 이렇게 다양한 영어책을 접할 수 있도록 해 주어야 한다. 다음은 영미권 아동 문학사에서 큰 위치를 차지하고 있는 여러 아동 문학상에 대해 정리한 것이다.

(www.helloknj.com에서 발췌)

Newbery Medal 	John Newbery(1713~1767)는 어린이의 수준과 흥미에 맞는 책들을 보급하는 데 큰 공헌을 한 영국의 출판업자로, 그가 활동했던 18세기에는 어린이들이 읽을 만한 책이 많지 않았다. 이런 시기에 John Newbery는 「*플루타크 영웅전*」, 「*영국의 역사*」, 「*마더구스 멜로디*」와 같은 어린이들을 위한 책을 출판해서 미국에까지 이름을 알리게 되고, 1922년 미국도서관협회는 아동 문학의 발전에 공헌한 Newbery의 이름을 붙여 아동문학상을 만들게 된다. Newbery Medal은 소설, 시집, 논픽션 부분에 걸쳐 상을 수여하는데 최고 작품에는 Newbery Medal의 영예가, 아쉽게 차점에 머무른 도서에는 Newbery Honor가 주어진다. 그 다음 상은 Silver, Bronze로, Newbery Medal은 여러 민족과 문화에 대한 이야기를 골고루 수상작에 포함시켜 인디언이나 에스키모의 생활, 한국이나 중국 등 여러 나라의 역사나 문화에 대한 이해를 돕고 있다.
Caldecott Medal 	Randolph Caldecott(1846~1886)은 영국의 그림 작가로 미술을 좋아했지만 은행원으로 사회생활을 시작했다. 그러나 그림에 대한 미련을 버리지 못하고 야간 예술학교에 다니며 그림 공부를 했고 스물여섯 살에 그림 작가가 된다. 그러다 1878년에 출판된 「*The House of that Jack Built*」와 「*The Diverting History of John Gilpin*」이 엄청난 인기를 끌었고 그 후로 매년 두 권 이상의 책을 출판하게 된다. 이렇게 그가 직접 글을 고르고 삽화를 그린 Nursery Rhymes 시리즈는 총 867,000권이나 팔렸고, 미국도서관협회는 1938년부터 아동 서적에서 가장 뛰어난 그림을 그린 작가에게 Caldecott Medal을 수여했다. 선발된 다섯 작품 중 최고 작품에는 Caldecott Medal을, 나머지 네 권에는 Caldecott Honor를 수여한다.

Kate Greenaway Medal 	Kate Greenaway(1846~1901)는 Randolph Caldecott과 비슷한 시기에 활동했던 영국의 인기 그림 작가로 그녀가 그린 「*Under the Window*(1878)」, 「*Marigold Garden*(1885)」 등의 작품은 엄청나게 인기를 끌었고, 그녀의 작품에 나오는 어린 소녀들의 옷이 유행을 하기도 했다. 1995년 영국도서관협회(Library Association)에서는 Kate Greenaway의 업적을 인정하여 동화책의 그림 분야에 기여한 작가에게 주는 상의 명칭으로 그녀의 이름을 붙였다. Kate Greenaway Medal은 2002년부터 도서정보전문공인협회(Chartered Institute of Library and Information Professionals)에서 주관하고 있는데 수상자는 금메달과 500파운드 상당의 책을 받아 자신이 선택한 도서관에 기증할 수 있다.
Nestle Children's Book Prize 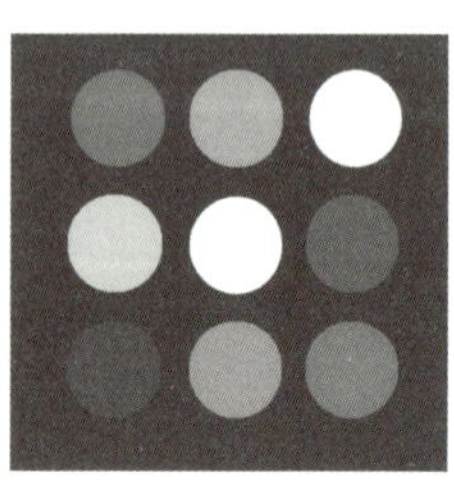	1985년부터 시작한 영국의 대표적인 아동문학상으로, 심사위원들이 먼저 후보작을 정하고 영국의 어린이들이 투표하여 수상작을 결정한다. 아이들이 뽑은 인기상이라고 할 수 있다. J. K. Rowling(Harry Potter), Jacqueline Wilson(Lizzie Zipmouth) 등의 인기 작가를 배출했고, 5세 이하, 6~8세, 9~11세의 세 부분으로 나누어 Gold, Silver, Bronze Medal을 수여한다.
The Golden Kite Awards 	1973년에 제정된 미국의 아동문학상으로 미국의 도서 작가와 일러스트레이터협회(Society of Children's Book Writers and Illustrators)가 주관하는 이 상은 소설, 비소설, 그림책 작가와 그림책삽화 작가 부분을 시상하고 있다.

Parents' Choice Awards 	미국의 비영리 단체인 Parents 'Choice Foundation(학부모협회)에서 1978년부터 수여하기 시작한 Parents' Choice Awards는 도서뿐만 아니라 오디오, 잡지, TV, DVD, 비디오 게임, 웹사이트 등 다양한 분야에 걸쳐 수상작을 결정한다. 상의 종류로는 Gold, Silver, Recommended, Approved Medal이 있다.
Boston Globe–Horn Book Awards 	이 상을 주관하고 있는 The Horn Book은 1924년 설립되었고 아동, 청소년 문학잡지(The Horn Book Magazine, The Horn Book Guide)를 발행하여 아동 문학에 선구적인 역할을 하고 있는 단체로 Boston Globe–Horn Book Awards는 1967년 제정되어 그림책, 소설과 시, 비소설 부뷰에 걸쳐 시상하고 있다. 상의 종류로는 Winner, Honor, Fanfare Honor List, Fanfare Selection 등이 있다.

▣ 책의 분류(Genre)

독립된 읽기(Independent Reading)를 할 때 다음의 분류를 참고해서 한쪽에 치우치지 않고, 다양한 장르의 글을 읽도록 지도해야 한다.

Fiction(소설)	Nonfiction(비소설)
Tell about imaginary people and events	Tells about real people and events
• Folklore : 작가 미상으로 오랜 세월 동안 여러 세대를 거쳐 구전되어 온 이야기	• Biography 중요한 인물의 삶에 대해 쓴 글
• Fantasy : 실제로는 일어날 수 없는 이야기나 사건	• Expository/Informative 사실과 정보를 주기 위해서 쓴 글
• Fairy Tale : 요정, 마법사와 같은 요소가 담긴 이야기	• Essay 어떤 주제를 개인적 시각으로 쓴 글
• Humor or Comedy : 재미있고 즐거운 이야기	• History 과거의 사건이나 시대에 관한 기록
• Mystery : 끝부분에 숨겨둔 비밀이 드러나는 이야기	• Journal 매일 매일의 사건에 관한 기록
• Drama : 배우들이 연극을 할 수 있도록 씌어진 글	• News Story 신문이나 잡지에서 볼 수 있는 보고문
• Adventure : 영웅과 악당이 나오는 이야기	• Reference 신속한 연구를 위해 유용한 사실과 정보를 체계적으로 정리하여 모아놓은 글
• Science Fiction : 우주나 미래에서 벌어지는 이야기	
• Historical Fiction : 과거속의 사람의 삶에 대한 이야기	

4 읽기에 대한 결론 및 당부의 말

우리나라와 같은 EFL 환경에서 책읽기는 매우 중요한 영어습득 방법이다. 학생들은 책을 읽으면서 어휘력, 독해력, 말하기, 듣기, 쓰기 능력이 향상되며, 더 나아가서 관심 있는 분야의 지식도 습득될 뿐만 아니라 개개인의 성장에도 도움이 된다. 따라서 교사와 학교는 학생들이 손쉽게 영어책을 읽을 수 있도록 환경을 마련해 주어야 한다. 특히, 교사는 학생들의 관심과 흥미를 불러일으킬 수 있는 주제나 쉽게 읽을 수 있는 책을 소개해 주고, 교실에는 책이나 읽을거리를 많이 배치해야 하며, 읽기 코너를 따로 마련해서 학생들의 책도 전시하고, 학습 게시판에 글을 부착해 두어 읽기 능력을 향상시킬 수 있는 분위기를 조성하여야 한다. 또 하나 당부하고픈 것은 교사 자신도 영어책을 많이 읽어야 한다는 것이다. 한 연구결과(Elly 1991)에 의하면 영어가 모국어가 아닌 교사들이 소리 내어 읽기(Reading Aloud)나 함께 읽기(Shared Reading) 프로그램을 통해서 영어에 대한 자신감을 얻었다고 보고 된 바 있다. 따라서 교사 자신이 스스로 독서에 대한 모범을 보이고, 학생들과 함께 어울려 책을 읽고, 서로 의견을 나누는 시간을 갖는다면 책읽기는 학생들과 교사 모두에게 즐거운 경험이 될 것이다.

MEMO

Part Ⅲ
쓰기(Writing)란 무엇인가?

1. 쓰기의 발달 단계(Stages of Writing Development)
2. 쓰기 과정(Writing Process)
3. 쓰기 구성 요소(Writing Components)
   1) 모범적 쓰기(Modeled Writing)
   2) 함께 쓰기 (Shared Writing)
   3) 유도된 쓰기(Guided Writing)
   4) 독립적 쓰기(Independent Writing)
4. 쓰기에 대한 결론 및 당부의 말

언어는 듣기, 말하기, 읽기, 쓰기 네 가지 영역으로 나눈다. 이 중에서 우리 아이들에게 가장 취약한 영역은 쓰기이다. 그 이유는 아이들이 영어로 글을 쓸 기회는 매우 적고, 영어로 글쓰기를 배워야겠다는 필요성을 느끼지 못하고 있기 때문이다. 또한 영어를 가르치는 교사 자신도 글쓰기에 대한 체계적인 지식을 가지고 있지 못하고, 또 영어로 자주 글을 쓰지 않기 때문에, 글쓰기를 왜 가르쳐야 하는지, 어떻게 가르쳐야 하는지 모르는 경우가 많다. 그러나 21세기에서 가장 중요하게 다뤄지고 있는 분야는 바로 글쓰기이다. 이제 쓰기(writing)에 대해 자세히 알아보자.

Part Ⅲ 쓰기란 무엇인가?

1 쓰기의 발달 단계(Stages of Writing Development)

쓰기의 발달 단계는 크게 6단계로 이뤄진다(Sulzby, 1985). 처음 단계는 그림그리기(drawing) 단계이고, 그러다가 낙서처럼 끄적거리는 단계(scribbling)를 지나, 철자와 비슷한 형태(letter-like forms)로 발전한다. 그 후에는 알파벳 철자(letter strings)를 쓰기 시작해서 문장을 쓸 때는 자신이 개발한 철자(invented spelling)를 사용하기도 한다. 이런 단계를 지나서 드디어 제대로 된 쓰기(conventional spelling)를 하게 된다. 각각의 단계는 서로 겹쳐져 나타나기도 하고, 또한 아이들마다 각 단계에 도달하는 시기는 각기 다르다.

Stage	Example
Drawing	
Scribbling	
Letter-like forms	
Letter strings	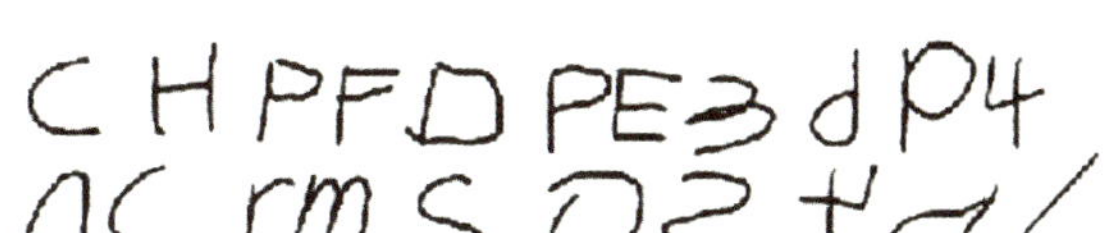

Invented spelling	I wl b hape wen skul iz t I lk t pla wt mi fredz in te sumr tatz l+z ov fn
Conventional spelling	Once upon a time a dog named Rags got lost in the woods. All of the people looked for him After a while he found his way home again His family was very happy.

2 쓰기 과정(Writing Process)

글을 쓸 때는 차근차근 단계를 거치면서 완성하게 된다. 이를 일컬어 쓰기 과정(writing process)이라고 하는데, 크게 5단계로 나눌 수 있다. 각 단계에 대해 알아보자. (각 단계의 예시 자료는 http://www.schenectady.k12.ny.us/에서 발췌했다.)

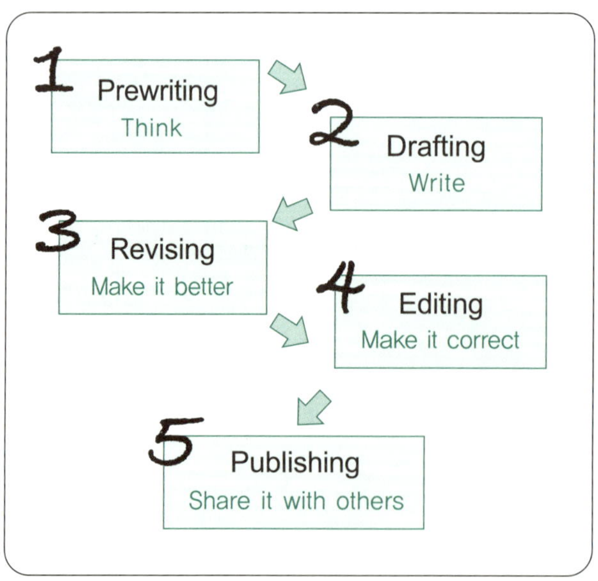

1) 쓰기 준비하기(Prewriting: Think)

쓰기 준비하기(prewriting)는 쓰기과정(writing process)의 다섯 단계 중에서 가장 중요한 단계 중의 하나로, 글을 쓰기 전에 아이디어를 얻는 단계라고 할 수 있다. 이때 아이디어를 얻는 방법으로는 브레인스토밍(brainstorming), 토론(discussion), 개요 짜기(outline), 벤다이어그램(venn diagram), 의미지도(making a web)를 이용하거나 관련 서적을 읽어 보기 등이 있다. 이렇게 해서 얻은 아이디어 중에서 주제와 무관한 것들은 삭제한 후, 글의 제목을 결정한다.

다음에 제시된 것은 사자(lion)에 관한 글을 쓸 때 어떻게 쓰기 준비하기(prewriting)를 하는지 브레인스토밍(brainstorming)한 것이다.

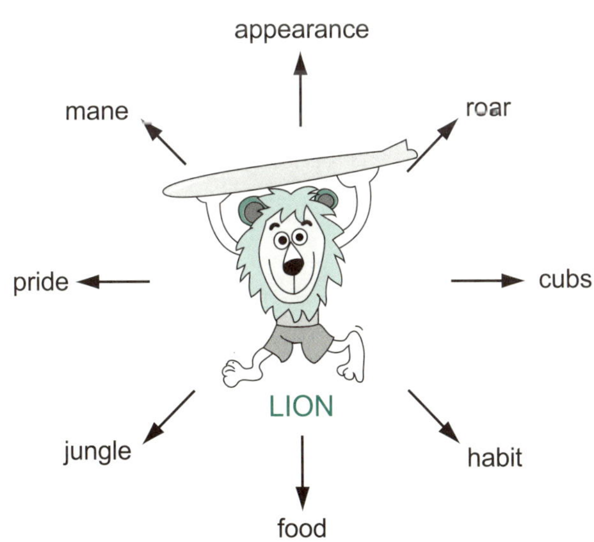

이렇게 브레인스토밍(brainstorming)을 한 후 다음과 같은 개요(outline)를 짠다.

Lions

I. Introduction

II. Appearance
- A. Normally tawny yellow, but color varies from gray to black.
- B. Female lion has paler coloring, especially on throat and belly.
- C. Long mane found only on male lion.
- D. Length of the lion's body is about six feet.

III. Habitat and Family Structure
- A. Lions live in groups called 'prides.'
- B. Pride is made up of one or more males, females, cubs, and adolescents.
- C. Live in the grasslands of Africa.

IV. Diet and Hunting Style
- A. Eats zebras and various types of deer.
- B. Hunts mainly at night, but is also active during cooler parts of the day.
- C. Hunts by ambushing prey.
- D. Several lions work together to capture prey.
- E. Lioness may hunt alone.
- F. Prey is usually killed by a single blow which breaks its spinal column.

V. Conclusion

2) 초안 쓰기(Drafting: Write)

초안 쓰기(drafting)는 쓰기 준비하기(prewriting) 과정에서 나온 아이디어를 바탕으로 글을 써 나가는 단계이다. 이 때 중요한 것은 내용(content)이기 때문에, 철자나 구두점과 같은 것은 신경 쓰지 않아도 된다. 또 글을 쓸 때는 교정을 볼 때 편하게 하기 위해서 문장 사이 간격을 넉넉하게 둔다. 다음은 사자에 대해 쓴 첫 번째 글(rough draft)이다.

Rough Draft
Lions

The lion is a massive african animal. The lion has long been considered the king of the grasslands because of its size. It live and hunts in a unique group, and is a carniverous animal. Its body is about six feet in length. the lions coat is normally tawny yellow.

The color varies from yellowish-gray to yellowish-black. Female lion has paler coloring.

The long main is found only on male lion. Lions live in groups called prides. A pride is made up of one or more males, one or more females, cubs and adolescents. Most lions live in the grasslands of Africa.

3) 수정하기(Revising: Make it better)

수정하기(revising) 과정은 써놓은 글을 다시 읽어 보면서 필요한 글을 추가하거나, 없애거나, 다시 재편성하면서, 글의 순서(beginning, middle, ending)가 옳게 되었는지 체크하고, 좀 더 자세하게 추가할 내용을 적는 과정이다. 또 접속사(and, but, because)를 사용해서 문장을 매끄럽게 연결한다. 수정하기(revising) 과정에서는 철자나 문법적인 것은 고치지 않는다.

Revision
Lion

The lion is a massive african animal. The lion has long been considered the

and strength

king of the grasslands because of its size ∧. It live and hunts in a unique

the lion — because it eats only other animals.

group, and ∧ is a carniverous animal ∧ .

The lion is an attractive and powerful animal.

∧ Its body is about six feet in length. The lions coat is normally tawny yellow. The color varies from yellowish-gray to yellowish-black. the female

especially on her throat and belly

lion has paler coloring ∧. The long main is found only on male lion.

Lions live in groups called prides A pride is made up of one or more males, one or more females, cubs and adolescents.

Most lions live in the grasslands of Africa.

Balanced Approach를 활용한
21세기 초등영어 지도방법

이러한 수정 작업은 혼자서 보는 것 보다는 여러 사람의 손을 거치는 것이 좋은데, 다음과 같은 도표를 활용하면 보다 효율적이다.

▣ 수정 요약리스트(Revising Summary)

REViSiNG SUMMARY

Tittle :

Here are some revisions I made :

1

2

3

4

5

I got revision ideas from(check all that apply) :

..........myself..........friend..........teacher conference

..........team conference..........brother / sister..........Mom / Dad

Signed : Date :

4) 편집하기(Editing: Make it correct)

이 단계에서는 철자(spelling), 대문자(capitalization), 구두점(punctuation) 그리고, 문법(grammar)이 맞는지 체크한다. 특히 이 과정은 혼자보다는 파트너와 서로 교환해서 체크하는 것이 더 좋다. 철자를 체크할 때는 교실 벽에 붙은 단어(word walls)나 사전(dictionaries)을 이용한다. 다음은 편집과정에서 사용하는 교정부호들이다.

■ 교정부호 (Editing Marks)

Symbol	Meaning	Example
lowercase	/	She Went to the park.
capitalize	≡	susan has three dogs.
delete		Tom likes the the lions.
misspelled word	○	Kevin cot the ball. (cought)
new paragraph		John went to sleep late last night. The next day, John walked to school
add/insert	∧	We had soup ∧ dinner. (for)
move		she ate at the circus cotton candy.
combine two words or parts		I saw some thing.
insert space	#	She likes chocolate icecream. (#)
insert missing punctuation	○	Kelly asked, "Where are you going" (?)

▣ 단어벽 꾸미기(Word Walls)

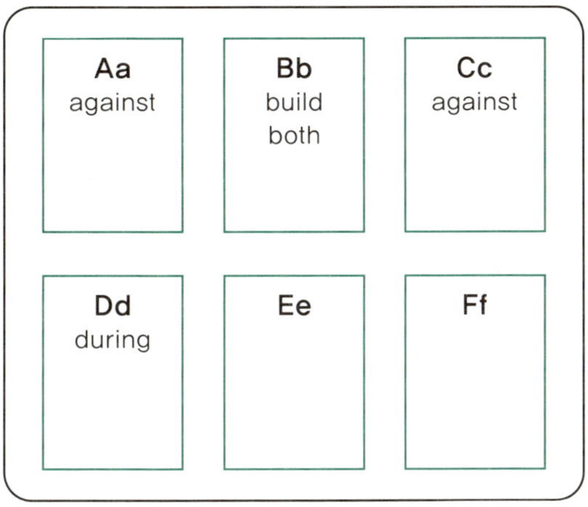

Word wall 이란 교실 벽면에 단어를 체계적으로 비치한 것을 말하는데, 아이들이 손쉽게 접근할 수 있어야 하며, 눈에 잘 띄게 만들어야 한다. 이 작업은 1년 동안 계속되며, 총 단어 수가 120개를 넘지 않도록 하는 것이 좋다. Word walls에 쓸 단어로는 빈도수가 높은 단어(high frequency words)나, 아이들이 철자를 잘 틀리는 단어, 철자 패턴(spelling pattern)이 있는 단어에서 고른다. 필요에 따라 단어를 추가하기도 하고, 있던 단어를 삭제하기도 한다. 또, 아이들 개개인이 자신만의 폴더를 준비해서 나만의 word wall을 만드는 것도 좋다. 다음은 high frequency words와 spelling pattern words를 정리한 것이다.

WORD LISTS

short *a*	short *e*	short *i*	short *o*	short *u*
apple animal after snacks class	everyone explain enter dressed pencil	interest invent dinner insect	strong clock beyond	under uncle unless understand
long *a*	**long *e***	**long *i***	**long *o***	**long *u***
disobey entertainment explain gray mailman painting player ray remaining waist yesterday	teacher speaker leave breeze between believe	tonight bright delight frightened excitement	grown borrowed unknown following shoulder dough though coastline throat soaking thorough	chewing screwdriver newspaper knew threw through regroup argument confuse truth congratulations
silent *e*	***ch, sh***	**soft *c*, hard *c***	***th, wh***	***bl, br, cl, cr, dr***
airplane suppose dispute gate alive upside true complete stripe illustrate	children change achievement reach teacher inches shower ashamed seashore pushed shivering	certain circle silence decide entrance country crayon welcome traffic cousin comparison	birthday thankful author another thousand together while whisper anywhere whichever worthwhile	bolck blanket library breakfast bridge closet clothing crown cradle drawer drinking

WORD LISTS

contractions	hard *g*, soft *g*	*fl, fr, gl, gr*	*oi, oy*	compound words
does't	grandfather	flvor	avoid	textbook
you're	goat	flight	moisten	football
would've	gallon	fraction	poison	everybody
we'll	garden	freedom	voice	afternoon
I'm	grateful	freeze	bolling	toothbrush
won't	giraffe	glance	rejoice	mailbox
shouldn't	general	gloves	destroy	raincoat
there's	gentle	ground	royalty	suitcase
areni't	giant	graphong	enjoyment	doorway
let's	genuine	grades	loyal	homesick
	generosity		annoyance	extraordinary

y as a vowel	double consonants	prefixes	suffixes	*y* to *ies*
suddenly	dollar	unwilling	happiness	babies
heavy	little	unknown	neatness	pennies
fearfully	tomorrow	disappear	colorful	hobbies
nursery	clapping	incorrect	hopeful	families
pretty	bottom	rebuild	wonderful	stories
buyer	mattress	rewrite	beautiful	fairies
myself	stubborn	redecorate	careless	dictionaries
dryness	arrange	prevent	agreement	
crying	effort	prepaid	loveable	
flyer	winner	midnight	noticeable	
technology	possibility	disappointment	greenish	

– tch	*pu, ph*	silent *kn, wr, gh*	*oo*	*ow, ou*
scratch	question	knife	moonlight	drowsy
patch	quarter	knees	balloon	crowded
matching	quiet	knock	afternoon	powerful
catcher	quarrel	knowledge	loose	allowance
batch	quality	wrong	bedroom	frown
fetch	earthquake	wrapper	bookmark	fountain
	phrase	wrinkle	looking	shout
	alphabet	wrist	stood	mouthful
	telephone	wrestling	crooked	round
	photograph	enough	cookie	lousy
	phonics	laughter	neighborhood	outstanding

HIGH-FREQUENCY WORD LISTS

able	boat	draw	go
above	body	dry	going
across	book	during	gold
add	both	early	gone
again	bottom	earth	good
against	box	easy	got
ago	boy	eat	great
air	bring	either	green
almost	brought	else	ground
alone	build	end	group
already	built	English	grow
also	came	enough	half
although	cannot	even	hand
always	can't	ever	happened
am	car	every	hard
American	care	everyone	head
among	carefully	everything	hear
animal	carry	example	heard
another	center	face	heart
answer	certain	fact	heavy
any	change	fall	held
anything	check	family	help
area	children	far	here
around	city	fast	high
asked	class	father	him
away	close	feel	himself
back	cold	feet	his
ball	come	felt	hold
beautiful	common	few	home
became	complete	follow	horse
because	country	food	hot
become	course	foot	hour
before	cut	form	house
began	dark	found	however
begin	day	four	hundred
behind	deep	friend	ice
being	didn't	front	idea
below	different	full	I'll
best	distance	game	I'm
better	does	gave	important
between	dog	get	inside
big	done	girl	instead
black	don't	give	itself
blue	door	glass	job

HIGH-FREQUENCY WORD LISTS

just	new	rock	surface
keep	next	room	system
kept	night	round	table
kind	nothing	run	take
knew	notice	sad	talk
land	number	same	tall
language	off	sat	tell
large	often	saw	ten
last	oh	say	that's
later	old	school	themselves
lay	once	sea	thing
learn	open	second	think
learned	order	seen	third
least	other	sentence	those
leave	our	set	though
leaves	outside	several	thought
left	own	shall	three
less	page	ship	through
let	paper	short	tiny
letter	part	should	to
life	past	show	today
light	pattern	shown	together
line	perhaps	side	told
list	person	simple	too
live	picture	since	took
lived	piece	six	top
living	place	size	toward
longer	plants	sky	town
look	play	small	tree
low	point	snow	true
main	poor	someone	turn
man	possible	something	turned
map	power	soon	under
matter	probably	sound	understand
me	problem	space	United States
mean	put	special	until
men	question	stand	upon
might	quite	start	us
mind	rain	state	usually
miss	ran	stay	voice
money	read	still	walked
moon	reading	stood	want
morning	ready	stop	warm
mother	real	story	watch
move	really	strong	yes
much	red	study	yet
must	remember	such	young
name	rest	suddenly	
near	right	summer	
need	river	sun	
never	road	sure	

▣ 편집 체크리스트(Editing Checklist)

다음은 editing과정에서 사용할 수 있는 체크리스트이다.

Editing Checklist

Author :__________　　Student Editor : __________

Title :__________　　Date : __________

※ Carefully read your piece out loud. Then read each item below. Correct any mistakes you find, and initial the space next to the item. Then see a student editor for a final check.

	Author	Editor	Items To Check
1.	______	______	Title, name, and date are OK.
2.	______	______	I checked for words I left out.
3.	______	______	Right and left margins are OK.
4.	______	______	Paragraphs are indented.
5.	______	______	Each sentence is complete.
6.	______	______	There are no run-on sentences.
7.	______	______	Each sentence begins with a capital letter.
8.	______	______	Proper nouns are capitalized.
9.	______	______	Each sentence ends with the correct punctuation.
10.	______	______	Commas, apostrophes, and quotation marks are OK.
11.	______	______	I checked the spelling of circled words.

실제 editing을 과정을 거친 글쓰기의 예를 살펴보자.

Editing
Lion

The lion is a massive african animal. The lion has long been considered the

and strength

king of the grasslands because of its size ∧. It live ∧ and hunts in a unique

s

the lion because it eats only other animals.

group, and ∧ is a carniverous animal ∧ .

carnivorous

The lion is an attractive and powerful animal.

∧ Its body is about six feet in length. The lion's coat is normally tawny

yellow. The color varies from yellowish – gray to yellowish – black. the female

especially on her throat and belly

lion has paler coloring ∧. The long main is found only on male lion.

mane

Lions live in groups called prides ∧ A pride is made up of one or more males,

one or more females, cubs and adolescents.

Most lions live in the grasslands of Africa.

5) 출판하기(Publishing: Share it with others)

글쓰기의 마지막 단계 publishing은 작품을 대중과 함께 하는 것(having your work go public)으로, 글을 깨끗하게 다시 쓰거나, 타이프를 치고, 필요하다면 그림을 넣어 완성 본을 만든다. 이렇게 완성된 작품은 교실에 비치해서 다른 아이들이 읽어 보게 하거나, 따로 시간을 내서 함께 읽어 본다.

Final Copy
Lions

The lion is a massive African animal. The lion has long been considered the king of the grasslands because of its size and strength. It lives and hunts in a unique group. The lion is a carnivorous animal because it eats only other animals. The lion is an attractive and powerful animal. Its body is about six feet in length. The lion's coat is normally tawny yellow. The color varies from yellowish-gray to yellowish-black. The female lion has paler coloring especially on her throat and belly. The long mane is found only on male lion. Most lions live in the grasslands of Africa. Lions live in groups called prides. A pride is made up of one or more males, one or more females, cubs and adolescents.

■ 출판 체크리스트(Publishing Checklist)

다음은 제시된 것은 Publishing Checklist이다. (http://printables.scholastic.com/에서 발췌하였다.)

Publishing Checklist

Name : ____________________ Date : ____________________

Ideas

- ☐ Ideas make sense.
- ☐ Ideas grab my reader's attention.
- ☐ I have a main idea and sense of purpose.
- ☐ I have drawn from experience.
- ☐ I say something new or in a new way.
- ☐ Piece is full of interesting and important ideas.

Word Choice

- ☐ I use just the right word or phrase.
- ☐ After reading, words are still memorable.
- ☐ Words are accurately used.
- ☐ Words are chosen wisely, but I take risks.
- ☐ I know the language of the topic, but don't try to impress.
- ☐ Simple language is used effectively.

Organization

- ☐ Opening makes the reader want to keep reading.
- ☐ Writing has logical order pr pattern
- ☐ Story or main points are easy to follow.
- ☐ Readers is able to predict but sometimes surprised.
- ☐ Loose ends are tied up. The piece ends well.
- ☐ The piece doesn't end with "Now you know.." or "Then I awoke and it was all a dream."

Voice

- ☐ This sounds like someone I know wrote it.
- ☐ Writing has style and flavor.
- ☐ Piece reaches out and "pulls me in."
- ☐ Piece makes me feel a certain way.

Sentence Fluency

- ☐ Writing is smooth and easy on the ear.
- ☐ Writing is easy to read aloud.
- ☐ Sentence begin in a variety of ways.
- ☐ Sentence vary in length.
- ☐ Sentence do not feel choppy or go on aimlessly.

Convention

- ☐ Writing is clean and polished.
- ☐ Spelling is correct. Punctuation is accurate and makes reading easy.

☐ Capital letters are used correctly.

☐ Paragraphs are indented.

☐ Grammar is correct.

Presentation

☐ Writing is pleasing to the eye.

☐ Handwriting is easy to read, with good slant and

☐ Spacing, or appropriate font is used.

☐ White space and text are nicely balanced.

☐ Clarity is enhanced with title, side heads, page numbers, or use of bullets.

☐ Text and visuals (illustrations, charts, graphs, tables, etc.)are integrated well.

3 쓰기 구성 요소(Writing Components)

1) 모범적 쓰기(Modeled Writing)

(1) 모범적 쓰기(Modeled Writing)의 정의

Modeled Writing이란 교사가 아이들 앞에서 글쓰기 모습을 시범적으로 보여주는 것으로, 교사가 글을 쓰면서 하는 생각과 글을 쓰는 행동을 말로 표현함으로써 글쓰기 과정을 쉽게 이해할 수 있다.

(2) 모범적 쓰기(Modeled Writing)의 수업

실제 modeled writing 수업을 어떻게 진행하는지 그 예를 살펴보자.

> 교사는 'Mr. Martinez is visiting the Sun Room today.' 란 문장을 modeled writing하기로 결정했고, 티칭 포인트는 단어 사이에 일정한 간격을 유지하는 것에 초점을 두었다. 교사는 칠판에 글을 쓰기 시작하면서, 자신이 하는 행동 하나하나를 말로 표현한다.
>
> T : I' m beginning in the top left corner. I write Mr. with a capital M and an r with a period. This is an abbreviation for the word Mr.
> (왼쪽 코너 위쪽에서 시작할게요. 먼저 Mr.를 쓸 텐데, 대문자 M과 소문자 r을 쓰고 온점(period)을 찍어요. Mr. 단어는 줄인 말이지요.)

T : I leave a space and write his name Martinez. It begins with a capital M, just like Margo's name.
(간격을 남겨두고, Martinez 이름을 씁니다. Martinez는 Margo처럼 대문자 M으로 시작합니다.)

T : I leave a space and write the next word is, like on our word wall.
(간격을 남겨두고 우리 word wall에 있는 것처럼 그 다음 단어 is를 씁니다.)

T : I leave a space and write the next word visiting. Visiting begins like Veronica with a v.
(간격을 남겨두고, 그 다음 단어 visiting을 씁니다. Visiting이란 단어는 Veronica처럼 v로 시작합니다.)

T : I leave a space and write the next word Sun. Sun looks like the word fun.
(간격을 남겨두고, 그 다음 단어 Sun을 씁니다. Sun은 fun이란 단어와 매우 비슷합니다.)

T : I leave a space and write the word Room. I leave a space and write the word today. I add a period at the end.
(간격을 남겨두고, 단어 Room을 씁니다. 간격을 남겨두고, 단어 today를 씁니다. 마지막에 온점(period)을 추가합니다.)

교사는 'Mr. Martinez is visiting the Sun Room today.' 란 문장을 큰 소리로 다시 한 번 읽어 준다. 그런 후 단어를 하나씩 짚어가면서 아이들과 함께 읽는다. 아이들이 복습을 할 수 있도록 문장을 지우지 않고 남겨둔다.

Modeled writing 수업 시간에 할 수 있는 또 다른 활동으로는 우리반 뉴스(class news)가 있다.

▣ 우리반 뉴스(Class News)

아이들에게 오늘 학교에서 일어났던 일에 대해서 생각을 해 보라고 한 후, 그 중에서 한 가지 일을 선택해서 차트에 적는다. 교사는 문장을 적으면서, 적는 행동 모두를 말로 표현한다. 예를 들어 대문자나, 구두점 혹은 다른 쓰기와 관련된 규칙이 있다면 이 모든 것을 말로 표현한다. 또 어떤 단어는 아이들에게 철자를 물어 보기도 한다. 문장이 완성되면 아이들과 함께 큰 소리로 읽어 본다. 필요하다면 그림을 추가하기도 한다. 이렇게 완성된 글과 그림은 'Our Class News' 라는 제목으로 책을 만든다.

MARCH 10. 2008
Today our class went to on a fleld trip to the zoo. We saw many animals.

▣ 대문자, 구두점 사용법(Mechanics)

Mechanics란 대문자 사용하는 법(capitalization)과, 구두점 찍는 법(punctuation)에 관한 규칙을 말한다. 이러한 규칙을 정확히 알고 있어야 제대로 된 글쓰기를 하게 된다.

대문자 쓰기 규칙(Rule for Capitalization)
• 문장의 시작은 대문자를 사용한다.(Use a capital at the beginning of a sentence.) 예 We went to the space center today.
• 편지글에서 인사로 시작하는 첫 단어와, 마무리 첫 단어는 대문자를 사용한다.(The first word in a greeting and the first word in a closing should be capitalized.) 예 Dear Mr. Jackson, Sincerely, Tamara
• 고유한 이름, 장소, 물건의 명사 이름과 모든 고유명사는 대문자로 시작한다.(A proper noun names a particular person, place, or thing. Every proper noun begins with a capital letter.) 예 Jacob, Center Middle School, Jupiter, Teen Magazine

• 엄마 아빠나 이름과 같이 쓰는 친척이름은 대문자로 쓴다.(The names of relatives, such as Father and Mother, should be capitalized when they are used as a name or with other name.) 예 Is Mother how yet? Did Uncle Jim call?
• Doctor와 같은 직함의 첫 글자나 Mrs와 같은 칭호의 축약형은 대문자로 쓴다.(The first letter of titles and abbreviations of titles, such as Doctor and Mrs., should be capitalized.) 예 Doctor Sanchez Mr. Sanchez
• 사람의 이름의 첫 글자는 대문자를 쓴다.(Use a capital letter for initials that stand for someone's name.) 예 J. F. Kennedy F. D. Roosevelt
• 모든 도시의 이름은 대문자로 시작한다.(Every city name begins with a capital letter.) 예 San Diego Jacksonville
• 모든 주의 이름은 대문자로 시작한다.(Every state name begins with a capital letter.) 예 Florida Michigan
• 요일이나 달은 대문자로 쓴다.(The days of the week and the months of the year each start with a capital letter.) 예 Friday January
• 휴일은 대문자로 시작한다.(The names of holidays begin with capital letters.) 예 President' s Day Memorial Day
• 책 제목에서 첫 단어, 마지막 단어, 그리고 중요한 단어는 대문자로 시작한다. 그러나 an, a, and, at by, for, in of는 제목의 첫 번째 단어로 올 때를 제외하고는 대문자로 쓰지 않는다.(The first word, last word, and each important word in a book title begin with capital letters. Do not capitalize words like an, a, and, at, by, for, in, of and the unless they are the first word or the title.) 예 Huckleberry Finn Trumpet of the Swans

• 단어 I 는 항상 대문자로 쓴다.(The word I is always capitalized.)

예 Dave and I are going to the movies this afternoon.

• 행성으로 Earth를 쓸 때는 대문자로 쓰지만, 대지란 뜻으로 쓰일 때는 대문자로 쓰지 않는다.(When referring to the planet, Earth is capitalized. When referring to dirt, it is not capitalized.)

예 I enjoy studying about our planet. Earth, and its moon.
The earth was dry and hard, so we used shovels to loosen the soil.?

구두점(Punctuation)

Comma(,)

• 서두에 나온 단어나 구 뒤에 쉼표를 쓴다. (Use a comma after introductory words or phrases.)

예 Chris, I found your missing necklace.
If we hurry, we can get to the bus stop in time.

• 중문에서 쉼표를 써서 문장을 분리시킨다.(Use a comma a compound sentence - two complete thoughts joined by and, but, or, yet, or for.)

예 The rain pored outside the tent, but we were snug and dry in our sleeping bags.

• 셋 이상 연속적으로 나열되었을 경우 쉼표를 써서 구분해 준다.(Use a comma to separate three or more phrases in a series.)

예 Did you vacations at the beach, in the mountains, or on the ranch?

• 독자에게 잠깐 쉬라고 하거나, 앞서 언급한 말과 사람의 이름을 분리시킬 때 쉼표를 사용한다. (Use a comma to tell the reader to pause, or to separate the name of the person being spoken to from what is being said.)

예 Brandon, are you coming with us?
Yes, my mom said I could go.

- 날짜와 연도 사이에 쓰거나, 년도 뒤에 문장이 계속 나오면 년도 뒤에 쓴다. (Use a comma in a date between the day of the month and the year, and after the year if the sentence continues.)

  예 My birthday is October 30, 1992.
  On February 9, 1992, my little sister was born.

- 도시와 주 사이, 주 뒤에 문장이 계속 될 경우 쉼표를 쓴다. (Use a comma between the city and the state, and after the state if the sentence continues.)

  예 Kelly lives in Lexington, Kentucky
  Kelly has lived in Lexington, Kentucky, for two years.

- 편지의 처음과 끝에 쉼표를 사용한다.(Use a comma after the greeting and the closing in a friendly letter,)

  예 Dear Uncle Bob,
  I hope you are felling much better.
  Sincerely, Naomi

- 비즈니스 편지의 끝에 쉼표를 사용한다.(Use a comma after the closing in a business letter.)

  예 Yours truly,
  Samuel Foster

Semicolon(;)

- 중문에서 두 개의 독립된 절은 연결할 때 세미콜론을 사용한다.(Use semicolon to combine two independent clauses in a compound sentence)

  예 Frank plays tennis; his sister is a swimmer

Colon(:)

• 리스트를 소개하거나, 물건들을 나열할 때 사용한다.(Use a colon to introduce a list or a series of things.)

예 For the hike, you will need the following items: sturdy shoes, thick socks, a water bottle, and a backpack.

• 다음과 같은 표현, 즉 for example, namely, for instance, that is 뒤에서 나열을 할 때는 콜론을 사용하지 않는다.(Do not use a colon if the series follows an expression, such as for example, namely, for instance, or that is.)

예 We were pestered by flying insects, namely mosquitoes and black flies.

• 시간을 쓸 때 시간과 분을 분리할 때 쓴다.(Use a colon to separate hours and minutes when writing the time.)

예 It is now 10:45 A.M.

• 비즈니스 편지의 서두나 인사말에 콜론을 쓴다.(Use a colon after the salutation or greeting in a business letter.)

예 Dear Mrs. Jennings :

Period(.)

• 평서문의 끝에 쓴다.(Use a period at the end of a statement.)

예 I love to write.

• 명령문의 끝에 쓴다.(Use a period at the end a command.)

예 Put the fried chicken in the picnic basket.

• 부탁하는 문장의 끝에 쓴다.(Use a period at the end a request.)

예 Please bring me that map.

• 축약형 뒤에 쓴다.(Use a period after abbreviations, such as Mrs., Ave., and yd.)

예 Mrs. Roberts lives on Sabrina Ave.

• 이름의 이니셜에 쓴다.(Use a period after an initial.)

예 U.S. Grant was a Civil War general before he become president.

Exclamation Point(!)

• 문장의 끝에 놀라움이나 경고의 뜻으로 느낌표를 쓴다.(Use an exclamation point at the end of a sentence that shows surprise or warning.)

예 Wow! you really surprised me just then.
Watch out for falling rocks!

Question Mark (?)

• 의문문의 끝에 물음표를 쓴다.(Use a question mark at the end of an interrogative sentence.)

예 Are you going to the football game tonight?

Quotation Mark (" ")

• 대화에 말을 정확하게 옮겨 적었을 때나, 말하는 사람의 이름이 먼저 나오고 그 뒤에 따옴표가 나오기 전에 쉼표를 쓴다.(Use quotations marks when writing exact words from a conversation. When the speaker's name comes first, use a comma before the quotations.)

예 Brent said, "That sounds really cool."

• 말하는 사람의 이름이 끝에 올 때 쉼표나, 느낌표, 물음표를 따옴표의 끝에 쓴다.(When the speaker's name comes last, use a comma, question mark, or exclamation point at the end of the quotation.)

예 "This is a special CD collection," answered Tony.
"Why are you wearing a sling?" asked Alyshia.
"Don't feed the bears!" warned Aaron.

• 말하는 사람의 이름이 가운데 올 때, 따옴표에서 이름을 분리하기 위해서 이름의 앞과 뒤로 쉼표를 쓴다.(When the speaker's name comes in the middle, use a comma before and after the name to separate it from the quotation.)

예 "Have you noticed," asked Julie, "that this playground is a mess?"

• 노래와 시, 노래의 제목에 따옴표를 쓴다.(Put quotation marks around the titles of songs, poems, and stories.)

예 "Yellow Submarine" by the Beatles
"Where the Sidewalk Ends" by Shel Silverstein
"The Emperor's New Clothes" by Hans Christian Anderson

Apostrophe (')

• 말을 줄 일 때 쓴다.(Use an apostrophe in a contraction to take the place of one or more letters that are taken away.)

예 can't, won't, shouldn't

• 누가 무엇을 소유하고 있을 때 쓴다.(Use an apostrophe in a possessive noun to show what belongs to whom.)

예 Sheila's shoes, the children's coats, the brothers's skateboards

2) 함께 쓰기(Shared Writing)

(1) 함께 쓰기(Shared Writing)의 정의

Shared Writing이란 교사와 아이들이 공동으로 글을 쓰는 것으로, 교사가 주도적으로 글쓰기를 하고, 아이들은 여기에 참여를 하게 된다. 이 때 교사는 다양한 글의 종류를 접하게 해 주어야 하며, 이 수업은 큰 규모의 그룹이나 작은 규모의 그룹 혹은 일대일 수업에도 적용이 가능하다.

(2) 함께 쓰기(Shared Writing)의 수업

실제 Shared Writing 수업을 어떻게 진행하는지 그 예를 살펴보자.

T : Let' s all say the story together.
(같이 이야기를 말해 봅시다.)

S : Here are the balls.
(Here are the balls.)

T : The first word is Here. What do you hear in Here?
(첫 단어는 Here입니다. Here에서 어떤 소리를 들을 수 있나요?)

S : *H*
(H)

T : Karen, you come up and write it on the chart. (Karen writes H.) What else do you hear, say it slowly, h-e-r-e. (Karen writes e r.) And there' s a silent e on the end, I will write it at the end. I have forgotten the next word. Let' s go back and say our sentence again.

(Karen 나와서 차트에 H를 써보세요. (Karen이 *H*를 쓴다.) here이란 단어를 천천히 말을 하면 어떤 것을 들을 수 있나요? (Karen이 *e*와 *r*을 쓴다.) 끝에 소리 나지 않는 e가 있어요. 내가 끝에 e를 쓸게요. 그 다음 단어를 잊어버렸네. 우리의 문장으로 돌아가서 다시 한 번 말해볼까요?)

S : Here are the balls.
(Here are the balls.)

T : Who can write the word are? (A hand goes up.) Billy, come write the word are. (Billy writes a r and the teacher fills in the e on the end.)
Let's read our sentence again from the beginning.
(누가 단어 are를 쓸 수 있나요? 한 명이 손을 든다. Billy 나와서 are를 써보세요. Billy가 ar을 쓰고, 교사는 단어의 끝에 e를 쓴다. 처음부터 다시 한 번 문장을 읽어봅시다.)

S : (Teacher points to each word as it is read.) Here are
(교사는 단어를 하나씩 지적한다.) (Here are……)

T : Who can write the word the? (Several hands go up.) Larry, come write the word the.(Larry writes the.) Let's read our sentence again from the beginning so we can remember what should come next.
(누가 그 다음 단어 the를 쓸 수 있나요?) (손을 든다.)(Larry, 나와서 단어 the를 쓰세요. Larry가 the를 쓴다. 다음에 어떤 단어가 나오는지 기억할 수 있게 처음부터 문장을 다시 읽어봅시다.)

S : (Teacher points to each word.)? Here are the
(교사는 단어를 하나씩 지적한다.) (Here are the……)

T : Balls. Who can write the first sound?(A hand goes up.) Carmen, come write the first sound. (Carmen writes b.) What else do you hear?
(Carmen says l and teacher acknowledges that there is an l, but explains that first there is an a, and teacher writes the a. Then Carmen writes the l and teacher fills in the other l.) Let's read our sentence again from the beginning.

(Balls. 누가 첫소리를 쓸 수 있나요? 한 명이 손을 든다. Carmen 나와서 첫 소리를 쓰세요. Carmen이 b를 쓴다. 또 어떤 소리를 들을 수 있나요? (Carmen이 l을 말하고, 교사는 l이 있지만 a가 먼저 나와야 한다는 것을 알려주고, a를 쓴다. 그런 후에 Carmen이 l을 쓰고 교사는 l을 한 번 더 쓴다.) 문장을 처음부터 다시 한 번 읽어봅시다.

S : (Teacher points to each word.) Here are the balls.

(교사는 단어를 하나씩 지적한다.) (Here are the balls.)

▣ 글쓰기 장르(Writing Genre)

함께 읽기(Shared Writing) 과정 중에 교사는 다양한 장르의 글쓰기를 유도해야 하는데, 다음은 이러한 글쓰기 장르를 정리 해 놓은 것이다.

Genre	Purpose
Descriptive Writing	서술문을 말하며, 아이들은 글을 쓰기 위해서 정확한 언어를 고르고, 조심스럽게 관찰하는 법을 배운다. 보다 강력한 글을 쓰기 위해서는 마치 눈앞에서 보이는 것처럼 생생하게 글을 써야 한다.
Expository Writing	설명문을 말하며, 독자에게 정보를 주거나 설명을 하기 위한 목적으로 쓴 글로, 아이들은 정보를 모으고, 종합하는 법을 배우게 된다. 대부분의 보고서(report)가 여기에 속한다.
Journals and Letters	일기나 편지글은 특정한 상대를 대상으로 쓴 글로, 다른 장르의 글보다 비공식적이다. 소식이나 새로운 생각을 알리거나, 기록을 남길 때 주로 사용되며, 특히 편지글의 경우는 편지와 봉투를 쓰는 방법을 따로 배워야 한다.
Narrative Writing	이야기 글을 말하며, 아이들은 자신에게 일어나는 사건에 관해 글을 써 보면서 Narrative Writing이 익숙해진다. 글을 쓸 때는 beginning, middle, end가 있어야 한다.

Persuasive Writing	설득문을 말하며, 다른 사람을 설득하기 위해 자신의 관점이나 생각을 구체적인 예와 증거를 들어 뒷받침해야 한다.
Poetry Writing	시를 말하며, 아이들은 시를 지으면서 언어란 생생하고 강력하지만 간결하다는 것을 배우게 되고, 동시에 시는 다양한 방법으로 배열할 수 있다는 것을 알게 된다.

▣ 일기쓰기(Journal)

일기(journal)라는 말은 '하루'를 뜻하는 라틴어 'diurnalis'에서 비롯되었다. 일기(journal)는 매일매일 발생한 사건들의 기록으로 다른 말로는 'daily diary'라고도 한다. 이런 일기 쓰기의 순서는 다음과 같다.

① 일기에 느낌과 생각을 쓸 것인지, 주요 사건을 기록할 지 아니면 두 내용을 다 담을 것인지 결정한다.

② 페이지 위쪽에 날짜를 적는다. 예) May 31, 2009

③ 그날의 일어난 가장 중요한 사건을 기록한다. 그리고 그 사건이 중요하다고 생각하게 된 이유를 설명하는 것도 좋다.

④ 가끔 일기를 읽어 본다. 어떤 특정한 날의 생각을 좀 더 넓고 깊게 표현하고 싶을지도 모르고, 생각이나 감정이 어떻게 변했는지를 기록하고 싶을지도 모르기 때문이다.

▣ 편지글 쓰기(Letter)

편지의 기본 양식은 두 가지로, 하나는 공식적인 편지 'formal letter' 또는 업무용 편지 'business letter'는 특정 정보를 요청하거나 제공하는 것으로 이러한 편지는 보통 잘 모르는 사람이나 알더라도 친구처럼 친하지 않은 사람에게 보낼 때 사용한다. 또 다른 하나는 사적인 편지 'personal letter'로 친구나 친척처럼 가까운 사이에 주고받는 편지를 말한다. 다음은 편지의 다섯 가지 기본 요소이다.

① 머리 부분 (Heading) : 날짜와 보내는 사람의 주소를 쓴다. 공적인 편지에서는 받는 사람의 이름과 주소도 써야 한다.

② 인사말(Greeting) : 편지를 받는 사람에게 간단하게 인사를 한다. 보통은 'Dear' 라는 말로 시작을 한다. 이 부분은 각 낱말의 첫 글자는 대문자로 써야하고, 사적인 편지에서는 인사말 끝에 쉼표(,)를 찍지만, 공적인 편지에서는 콜론(:)을 붙인다.

③ 본문(Body) : 본문은 편지의 내용을 쓰는데, 많은 사람들이 본문의 첫 줄을 들여 쓴다. 만약 첫 째 줄을 들여 썼다면 새로운 단락이 시작할 때마다 첫 줄을 들여 써야 한다.

④ 맺음말(Closing) : 업무용 편지에서는 맺음말로 Your truly, Sincerely, Regards 등의 정중한 표현을 사용하고, 사적인 편지에서는 좀 더 다정하고 친숙하게 들리는 Your friend, Affectionately, Love 등의 표현을 사용한다. 맺음말의 첫 글자는 대문자로 써야하며, 끝에는 쉼표(,)를 붙여야 한다.

⑤ 서명 (Signature) : 맺음말 밑에는 항상 서명(signature)을 해야 한다. 그리고 공적인 편지에서는 서명 밑에 또렷한 글씨로 이름을 적어 넣어야 한다.

⊙ 봉투 쓰는 법

⦿ 공적인 편지 (Business Letter)

보내는 사람 주소 → 207 Hope Street
Alpine, OR 97408

날 짜 → June 10, 2008

받는 사람 → Jenny Kim
Sirs Import and Export, Inc.

받는 사람 주소 → 64SEventh Street
New York, NY 10022

인사말, 뒤에 콜론을 붙여요. → Dear Sir :

본 문 → I have not yet received the three cartons of heirloom seeds. I ordered from your company three weeks ago. I would appreciate it if this problem could be taken care of as soon as possible.

맺음말, 뒤에 쉼표를 붙여요. → Sincerely,
Allan Baynes
Allan Baynes

⦿ 사적인 편지(Personal Letter)

날 짜 → Feb 16, 2008

인사말, 뒤에 쉼표를 붙여요. → Dear Miss Judy,

본 문 → Thank you so much for being my piano teacher. I feel like have learned so much over the past year. I really appreciate all the time you spent helping me get ready for the school talent show.
I'm sorry that we are moving and I won't get to be your student anymore. I'll miss our Tuesday practice. I promise I will keep in touch and let you know about my new teacher.

Thank again for all your help. I will miss you.

맺음말, 뒤에 쉼표를 붙여요. → Your Friend,
Casey

3) 유도된 쓰기(Guided Writing)

(1) 유도된 쓰기(Guided Writing)의 정의

Guided Writing 시간에 교사는 작은 그룹 혹은 일대일 수업을 통해 아이가 글쓰기를 할 수 있도록 촉진제 역할 및 안내자 역할을 하게 된다. 이 시간을 통해 아이들은 modeled writing과 shared writing 시간에 배운 것을 적용하여 되도록 교사의 도움 없이 혼자서 글을 쓰는 연습을 하게 된다.

(2) 유도된 쓰기(Guided Writing)의 수업

Guided Writing을 하기 전에, 교사와 아이들이 나눈 대화를 정리한 것이다.

Before Writing Sample Dialogue

T : In this guided reading session we are going to write a procedure. Who can remember what a procedure is?
(이번 guided reading session에서는 절차(procedure)가 있는 글을 써 봅시다. procedure가 무엇인지 기억할 수 있나요?)

S : It's a list of instructions.
(지시 순서를 나열한 것입니다.)

T : That's right. Do you remember, I wrote a procedure in modelled writing when I wrote down the recipe for chocolate crackers? We put it one the wall over there, so that we could use it I cooking. Then we all wrote a procedure in shared writing when we wrote the instructions for our new language game. Can anybody remember how we start a procedure?

(맞아요. 기억나나요? 내가 초콜릿 과자 만드는 방법을 적을 때, modelled writing을 하면서 procedure를 썼지요. 저 쪽 벽에 그 것을 붙여 놨어요. 그래서 우리가 요리를 할 때 그걸 보고 사용할 수 있지요. 그런 후에 shared writing시간에 새로운 언어게임을 위한 지도 방법을 적으면서 우리 모두 procedure를 썼어요. 누구 procedure를 어떻게 시작하는지 기억하는 사람 있나요?)

S : First of all we write the goal.
(우선 목표를 적어야 해요.)

T : Well done. Yes, we state what it is we are aiming to do. Then what?
(잘했어요. 네, 우리의 목표가 무엇인지 언급해 주어야 해요. 그런 다음엔 뭐지요?)

S : We make a list of things we' ll need.
(필요한 목록을 만들어야 해요.)

T : Good. After that?
(좋아요. 그 다음에는 무엇인가요?)

S : We write a list of steps that we need to take, one after the other. Sometimes we draw something to show how you do it.
(필요한 단계 목록을 하나씩 써요. 때로는 어떻게 해야 하는지를 보여주기 위해서 그림을 그리기도 해요.)

S : Then we wrote a sentence about what it should be like when you finish.
(그런 후에 끝나고 나면 어떻게 되어야 하는지 문장을 써요.)

T : Excellent. You really do remember how to write a procedure.
(훌륭해요. 여러분은 procedure를 어떻게 써야 하는지 기억하고 있군요.)

S : Anyway, we make a chart. didn' t we, with everything on it. Look, it' s on the wall over there.
(우리는 이미 모든 게 적혀 있는 차트를 만들었어요. 보세요. 벽에 있잖아요.)

T : Yes, we created a framework to guide us after we had read several procedures other people had written. So there' s lots of help around the room if you need it.

(네, 우리는 다른 사람이 쓴 procedures를 읽고 나서 우리만의 틀을 만들었어요. 그래서 우리 교실 주변에 있는 붙어 있는 그 틀이 여러분이 필요할 때 도움을 줄 수 있어요.)

T : The procedure we're going to write today in instructions about how to make a mask. We've been making masks in Art and Craft, so we all know exactly what to do. Don't forget that you can illustrate your instructions if you think it will make it easier for the other children.
(오늘 우리가 쓸 procedure는 어떻게 가면을 만들 수 있는가 하는 겁니다. 이미 미술 시간에 가면을 만들어 봤어요. 그래서 우리 모두는 어떻게 해야 하는지 정확하게 알고 있어요. 다른 사람들이 좀 더 이해를 쉽게 하기 위해서는 그림을 그려 넣을 수 있다는 것을 잊지 마세요.)

T : Today I think we'll work with a partner. Now that each pair has found a good spot, let's begin.
(오늘은 짝꿍과 작업을 함께 하세요. 이제 짝꿍과 함께 좋은 장소를 찾아서 시작하세요.)

During Writing Sample Dialogue

T : Who would like to read their opening statement?
(오프닝 멘트를 읽어 줄 사람 누구인가요?)

S : Me. 'Making a Mask. I am going to tell you how to make an animal mask.
(저요, '가면 만들기. 동물 가면을 어떻게 만드는지 알려드릴게요.')

T : That's a good title and opening statement. Anyone else?
(좋은 제목과 오프닝 멘트군요. 다른 사람 없나요?)

S : I will. 'Making Masks. Instructions for Making Masks.' Sam and I didn't know how to spell 'instructions', so we went to the chart on the wall and copied it.
(저요. '가면 만들기, 가면 만들기 지도법.' Sam과 저는 'instruction' 철자를 몰라서, 벽에 붙어 있는 차트를 보고 썼어요.)

T : That was a good thing to do. Well, we've had some excellent beginning statements, now let's write the next section. Remember, the next section tells the children what they are going to need. If you can't spell a word, be as resourceful as Sam and Tim and try to find it for yourselves before you ask me. 'Instructions' was a very hard word to spell. I'll certainly add it to our class wall bank of interesting words.
(정말 잘했어요. 모두 멋진 멘트로 시작을 했군요. 이제 다음 섹션을 써 봅시다. 기억하세요. 다음 섹션은 무엇이 필요한지 알려주어야 합니다. 만약 단어의 철자를 모른다면, Sam과 Tim처럼 선생님에게 물어 보기 전에 다른 자료들을 찾아보기 바랍니다. 'Instructions' 은 철자가 어려운 단어지요. 선생님도 그 단어를 우리 반 벽에 붙어 있는 단어에 추가해야겠어요.)

4) 독립적 쓰기(Independent Writing)

(1) 독립적 쓰기(Independent Writing)의 정의

Independent Writing이란 교사의 도움 없이 아이 혼자서 글을 쓰는 것을 말한다. 이 과정에서 아이는 단어벽(word wall)이나 차트, 사전, 컴퓨터 등을 사용할 수 있다. 아이들은 매일 적어도 10~15분씩 글쓰기 기회가 주어져야 한다. 이 시간을 통해서 아이들은 구어(written language)에 대한 이해의 폭이 넓어지게 된다. 또한 교사는 아이들이 독립적 쓰기(independent writing)하는 것을 참고로 해서, 모범적 쓰기(modeled writing), 함께 쓰기(shared writing), 유도된 쓰기(guided writing) 수업 내용에 반영할 수도 있다.

(2) 독립적 쓰기(Independent Writing)의 수업 활동

교사는 아이들이 다양한 경험을 통해서 글쓰기를 할 수 있도록 도와 주어야 한다. 예를 들어 지역축제나 박물관 방문 혹은 공연과 같은 체험을 한 뒤에 체험 순서라든가 개개인이 느낀 감정 등을 글로 나타내는 것도 좋은 활동 중의 하나이다.

또 아이들마다 작은 노트하나를 마련하게 한다. 이 노트의 이름을 작가의 공책(writer's notebook)이라고 한 후에, 아이들에게 자신이 작가라고 생각하고 이 노트에다 글을 쓰라고 한다. 글의 내용은 그림을 그려도 되고, 감정을 써도 되고, 떠오르는 재미난 이야기를 써도 되고 그 내용은 아이들 마음대로 선택해서 쓰게 한다. 처음에는 단순한 그림이나 이야기로 시작되지만, 노트가 채워질 무렵에는 어느새 우리 아이들의 영어 쓰기 실력은 향상되어 있을 것이다.

또 다른 활동 방법으로 교사는 공책과 작은 곰돌이 인형을 준비해서 가방에 넣는다. 이 가방의 이름을 글쓰기 가방(writing bag)이라고 한 후 매주 금요일에 순서를 정해서 아이들에게 가방을 전해 준다. 가방을 받은 아이는 곰돌이 인형을 가지고 어떤 일을 했는지 공책에 상세하게 글을 써야 한다. 예를 들어 곰돌이와 같이 차를 마셨거나, 동화책을 읽었거나, 목욕을 했거나, TV를 봤다는 등의 내용을 쓰게 한다. 시간이 흘러 반의 모든 아이들이 한 번 씩 글을 쓰게 되면 아이들과 함께 글의 내용을 가지고 이야기를 나눈다. 이 활동을 마칠 때쯤이면 아이들은 글쓰기 가방을 받는 금요일을 기다리고 있을 것이다.

4 쓰기에 대한 결론 및 당부의 말

어린아이는 적절한 언어 환경에 놓이게 되면 쉽게 말을 배운다. 생후 1년이 지나면 단어를 말하고, 시간이 지남에 따라 문장을 말하고, 문법과 구문을 터득하여 복잡한 묘사나 설명도 할 수 있게 된다. 그래서 특별한 장애가 없는 한, 어린이는 누구나 어렵지 않게 말을 배우게 된다. 이에 비해 쓰기는 상당히 많은 시간과 노력을 기울여서 어렵게 배운다. 마치 수영이나 자전거를 배울 때처럼 누군가의 도움과 별도로 마련된 학습 활동을 통해서 쓰기를 배운다. 또 모든 아이들이 성공적으로 쓰기를 배우는 것도 아니다. 일부 아이들은 결국 쓰기를 배우지 못하거나 사회에서 요구하는 수준까지 도달하지 못하는 경우도 있다. 이렇게 아이들이 쓰기를 쉽게 배우지 못하는 이유는 무엇일까? 그 이유 중의 하나는 쓰기 교육이 단편적이고 일관성이 없기 때문이다. 또 쓰기를 제대로 배우기 위해서는 장시간에 걸친 체계적인 지도와 연습이 필수적인데, 아이들은 이런 과정을 어렵고 따분하게 느끼는 경우가 많기 때문에 중간에 쓰기를 포기하는 경우가 많다. 따라서 교사는 아이들이 좋아하고 쉽게 이해 할 수 있는 의미 있는 활동으로 글쓰기 수업을 구성하여야 한다. 또한 영어를 가르치는 교사 자신부터 영작문에 대한 체계적인 지식을 갖추도록 노력해야 하며, 꾸준히 글을 써 보는 훈련을 해 봐야 한다. 근래에 이르러 쓰기에 대한 관심이 증가하고 있는 것은 무척 다행스러운 일이다. 이러한 시대의 흐름에 발맞추기 위해서라도 교사는 쓰기의 중요성을 인식하고, 아이들에게 쓰기를 꾸준히 시킬 수 있는지 늘 연구해야 할 것이다.

저자는 책 전체를 통해서 읽기, 쓰기의 중요성과 구체적 실천 방법을 강조하였다. 이제 책을 마무리하면서 또 한 번 강조하고 싶은 것은 읽기와 쓰기의 균형을 어떻게 맞추느냐는 것이다. 이 책에 제시된 기본 내용을 바탕으로 해서 아이들에게 읽기와 쓰기를 어떻게 연결시킬 것인지 연구하는 교사가 되길 바란다.

첨부자료

다음은 실제 교실에서 활용할 수 있는 자료들을 첨부하였다.

Nursery Rhyme Mini-Posters 1

Little Miss Muffet

Little Miss Muffet
Sat on a tuffet,
Eating her kurds and whey;
Along came a spider
Who sat down beside her
And frightened Miss Muffet away.

Mary, Mary, Quite Contrary

Mary, Mary, quite contrary,
How does your garden grow?
With silver bells snd cockle shells
And pretty maids all in a row.

Little Bo Peep

Little Bo Peep has lost her sheep,
And doesn' t know where
To find them;

Leave them alone and
They' ll come home,
Wagging their tails behind them.

Hickory, Dickory, Dock

Hickory, Dickory, Dock!
The mouse ran up the clock;
The clock struck one,
The mouse ran down,
Hickory, Dickory, Dock!

Nursery Rhyme Mini-Posters 2

Hey Diddle, Diddle

Hey Diddle, Diddle
The cat and the fiddle,
The cow jumped over the moon.
The little dog laughed
to see such sport,
And the dish ran away
with the spoon.

Pease Porridge

Pease Porridge hot,
Pease Porridge cold,
Pease Porridge in the pot,
nine days old.
Some like it hot,
Some like it cold,
Some like it in the pot,
nine days old.

Mary Had Little Lamb

Mary had little lamb,
Whose fleece was white as snow;
And everywhere that Mary went
The lamb was sure to go.

Jack and Jill

Jack and Jill went up the hill,
To fetch a pail of water.
Jack fell down, and
broke his crown,
And Jill came tumbling after.

Nursery Rhyme Mini-Posters 3

Baa, Baa, Black Sheep

Baa, Baa, black sheep,
Have you any wool?
Yes, sir, yes, sir,
Three bags full;
One for my master,
One for my dame,
And one for the little boy
Who lives down the lane.

The Old Woman Who Lived in a shoe

There was an old woman
Who lived in a shoe.
She had so many children,
She didn't know what to do.
She gave them some broth
Along with some bread,
Then huggod thcm
all soundly
And sent them
to bed.

The Itsy Bitsy Spider

The itsy bitsy spider
Climbed up the water spout.
Down came the rain
And washed the spider out.
Out came the sun
And dried up all the rain.
And the itsy bitsy spider
Climbed up the spout again.

Star Light, Star Bright

Star light, star bright
First star I see tonight,
I wish I may, I wish I might,
Have the wish I wish tonight.

다음은 그림으로 표현이 가능한 단어목록이다.

500 Picture Words

ant	boll	cave	cry	finger	grapes	inch
apple	bone	ceiling	cub	fire	graph	ink
ax	book	chain	cube	fish	grass	itch
baby	boot	chair	cup	flag	grasshopper	jacks
backpack	bow	chalk	cut	flashlight	green	jam
bag	bowl	check	dance	float	grill	jar
ball	box	cheese	deer	floor	groom	jet
balloon	boy	cherry	desk	flower	guitar	jug
banana	bread	chest	dice	flute	gym	juggle
band	brick	chimney	dig	fly	ham	jump
bank	bride	chin	dinosaur	fold	hammer	kangaroo
barn	bridge	chop	dive	foot	hand	key
baseball	broom	circle	dog	football	hat	kick
basket	brother	circus	doll	fork	hawk	king
bat	brown	city	door	forty	hay	kiss
bath	brush	clap	dot	four	heart	kit
beach	bug	clay	draw	fox	heel	kitchen
beak	building	cliff	dress	frame	hen	kite
bean	bun	clock	drip	fright	hide	knee
bear	bus	cloud	drum	frown	hill	knife
bed	bush	clown	duck	fruit	hippo	knock
bee	button	coat	eat	fry	hit	knot
beg	cab	coins	egg	game	hive	ladder
bell	cage	cold	elbow	garden	hole	lake
belt	cake	comb	elephant	gate	hop	lamp
bench	camel	cone	envelope	gift	horn	lap
bib	camera	corn	face	giraffe	horse	leaf
bike	can	cot	fall	girl	hose	leash
bird	candle	cow	fan	glass	hot	leg
black	cane	crab	feather	globe	house	lemon
block	cap	crawl	feet	glue	hug	letter
blow	car	crib	fence	goat	hump	lid
blue	carrot	crown	fifty	gold	hut	light
boat	cat	crutches	fin	goose	ice	line

lion	nose	pool	ruler	snow	thirty	volcano
lips	nurse	pop	run	soap	thorn	wagon
list	nut	popcorn	sand	sock	three	wallet
lock	octopus	porch	sandwich	spider	throw	wash
log	oil	pot	saw	spill	thumb	watch
lunch	ox	pretzel	scale	spin	tie	watermelon
mail	page	prize	scarf	spoon	tiger	wave
mailbox	pail	pumpkin	school	spray	tire	wax
man	paint	purse	seal	spring	toad	web
map	pan	puzzle	seed	square	toast	well
mat	paw	quack	seaven	squeeze	toe	wet
mask	pay	queen	shadow	squirrel	tooth	whale
match	peas	question	shark	stamp	top	wheel
meat	peach	quick	shave	star	toys	wheelchair
men	peel	quilt	sheep	steam	train	whistle
mice	pen	quiz	shell	steps	tray	white
milk	pencil	rabbit	ship	stir	tree	wig
mirror	penguin	rag	shirt	stop	triangle	window
mitt	pet	rain	shoe	strawberry	truck	wing
mitten	phone	rainbow	shoelace	street	trunk	worm
mix	photograph	rake	shorts	stump	tub	wrist
monkey	piano	rat	shout	suit	turkey	write
moon	pie	red	shovel	sun	turtle	yard
mop	pig	read	sink	sweep	twenty	yarn
mouse	pillow	right	sit	swim	two	yawn
mouth	pin	ring	six	swing	umbrella	yell
mule	pink	rip	skate	table	under	yellow
mushroom	plane	road	skirt	tack	up	yo-yo
music	plant	robe	skunk	tail	vacuum	yolk
nail	plate	robot	sled	tape	valentine	zebra
neck	plow	roof	sleep	team	van	zero
necklace	plug	roots	slice	teeth	vase	zigzag
needle	point	rope	smell	ten	vegetables	zipper
nest	pole	rose	smoke	tent	vest	zoo
night	pond	row	snail	thermometer	vine	
nine	pony	rug	snake	thirteen	violin	

The 500 Most Frequently Used English Word

1-25				
the	in	he	as	at
of	is	was	with	be
and	you	for	his	this
a	that	on	they	have
to	it	are	I	from
26-50				
or	but	we	there	she
one	not	when	use	do
had	what	your	an	how
by	all	can	each	their
word	were	said	which	if
51-75				
will	many	some	him	two
up	then	her	into	more
other	them	would	time	write
about	these	make	has	go
out	so	like	look	see
76-100				
number	my	call	find	get
no	than	who	long	come
way	first	oil	down	made
could	water	its	day	may
people	been	now	did	part
101-125				
over	little	live	very	name
new	work	me	after	good
sound	know	back	thing	sentence
take	place	give	our	man
only	year	most	just	think

126-150				
say	much	mean	boy	also
great	before	old	follow	around
where	line	any	came	form
help	right	same	want	three
through	too	tell	show	small
151-175				
set	well	such	ask	land
put	large	because	went	different
end	must	turn	men	home
does	big	here	read	us
another	even	why	need	move
176-200				
try	change	away	letter	still
kind	off	animal	mother	learn
hand	play	house	answer	should
picture	spell	point	found	American
again	air	page	study	world
201-225				
high	between	last	never	light
every	own	school	start	thought
near	below	father	city	head
add	country	keep	earth	under
food	plant	tree	eye	story
226-250				
saw	along	next	life	together
left	might	hard	always	got
don't	close	open	those	gourp
few	something	example	both	often
while	seem	begin	paper	run
251-275				
important	car	sea	four	hear
until	mile	began	carry	stop
children	night	grow	state	without

side	walk	took	once	second
feet	white	river	book	later
276-300				
miss	watch	let	cut	song
idea	far	above	young	being
enough	Indian	girl	talk	leave
eat	real	somethimes	soon	family
face	almost	mountain	list	it's
301-325				
body	questions	horse	knew	usually
music	fish	birds	since	didn't
color	area	problem	ever	friends
stand	mark	complete	piece	easy
sun	dog	room	told	heard
326-350				
order	top	short	hours	measure
red	ship	better	black	remember
door	across	best	products	early
sure	today	however	happened	waves
become	during	low	whole	reached
351-375				
listen	fast	five	true	table
wind	several	step	hundred	north
rock	hold	morning	against	slowly
space	himself	passed	pattern	money
coverd	toward	vowel	nummeral	map
376-400				
farm	cold	sing	town	field
pulled	cried	war	I'll	travel
draw	plan	ground	unit	wood
voice	notice	fall	figure	fire
seen	south	king	certain	upon

401-425				
done	fly	correct	shown	front
English	gave	of	minutes	feel
road	box	quickly	strong	fact
half	finally	person	verb	inches
ten	wait	became	stars	street
426-450				
decided	building	rest	stay	less
contain	ocean	carefully	green	machine
course	class	scientists	known	base
surface	note	inside	island	ago
produce	nothing	wheels	week	stood
451-475				
plane	boat	warm	though	yes
system	game	common	language	clear
behind	force	bring	shape	equation
ran	brought	explain	deep	yet
round	understand	dry	thousands	government
476-500				
filled	object	power	dark	fine
heat	am	cannot	ball	pair
full	rule	able	material	circle
hot	among	six	special	include
check	noun	size	heavy	built

Numbers

0	zero		
1	one	1st	first
2	two	2nd	second
3	three	4rd	third
4	four	4th	fourth
5	five	5th	fifty
6	six	6th	sixth
7	seven	7th	seventh
8	eight	8th	eighth
9	nine	9th	ninth
10	ten	10th	tenth
11	eleven	11th	eleventh
12	twelve	12th	twelfth
13	thirteen	13th	thirteenth
14	fourteen	14th	fourteenth
15	fifteen	15th	fifteenth
16	sixteen	16th	sixteenth
17	seventeen	17th	seventeenth
18	eighteen	18th	eighteenth
19	nineteen	19th	nineteenth
20	twenty	20th	tweentieth
21	twenty-one	21st	twenty-first
22	twenty-two	22nd	twenty-second
23	twenty-three	23rd	twenty-third
24	twenty-four	24th	twenty-fourth
25	twenty-five	25th	twenty-fivth
30	thirty	30th	thirtieth
31	thirty-one	31st	thirty-first
40	forty	40th	fortieth
41	forty-one	41st	forty-first
50	fifty	50th	fiftieth
60	sixty	60th	sixtieth

70	seventy	70th	seventieth
80	eighty	80th	eightieth
90	ninety	90th	ninetieth
100	one hundred	100th	one hundreth
150	one hundred fifty		
200	two hundred		
500	five hundred		
1,000	one thousand		
1,100	one thousand one hundred		
1,500	one thousand five hundred		
2,000	two thousand		
1,000,000	one million		one millionth
1,000,000,000	one billion		one billionth

Calendar Words

Days of the week	
Monday	Mon.
Tuesday	Tues.
Wednesday	Wed.
Thurday	Thurs.
Friday	Fri.
Saturday	Sat.
Sunday	Sun.

Month	
January	Jan.
February	Feb.
March	Mar.
April	Apr.
May	May
June	Jun.
July	Jul.
August	Aug.
September	Sept.
October	Oct.
November	Nov.
December	Dec.

Major Holidays	
New Year's Day	January 1
Valentine's Day	February 14
April Fool's Day	April 1
Parent's Day	May 8
Independence Day	August 15
Halloween	October 31
Christmas Day	December 25
New Year's Eve	December 31

Antonyms

above	below	high	low
add	subtract	in	out
all	none	left	right
always	never	light	dark
arrive	leave	long	short
back	front	lost	found
before	after	loud	soft
begin	end	love	hate
big	little	many	few
black	white	more	less
boy	girl	morning	evening
come	go	most	least
dark	light	near	far
day	night	new	old
dead	alive	old	new
deep	shallow	on	off
empty	full	open	close
even	odd	over	under
fast	slow	right	wrong
fat	thin	same	different
find	lose	sharp	dull
first	last	small	large
floor	ceiling	something	nothing
friend	enemy	start	stop
give	get	tall	short
go	stop	then	now
good	bed	to	from
happy	sad	together	apart
hard	soft	top	bottom
he	she	up	down
heaven	hell	wet	dry
heavy	light	with	without
here	there	yes	no

Thematic Language Units

Animals	Numbers
Types of animals Habitats of animals Pets Zoos	Ordinal Cardinal Number formats : decimal, fractions, etc.
Education	**Measurement**
Classroom vocabulary	Sizes Distances
Family	**Passage of time**
Names for family members	Time vocabulary Days of the week Months of the year Seasons Holidays
Food	**Shopping**
Names of food Names of meals Kitchen and table items Grocery shopping Going to a restaurant	Places to shop Names of clothing and accessories Colors
Health	**Social**
Body parts	Greetings Terms of respect Etiquette Entertainment and leisure activities
Housing	
Types of housing	

Punctuation

- apostrophe (') : the Kenny' s house : can' t
- colon(:) : 3:45 P.M.
- comma (,) : Yes, I like apples. March 1, 2009
- exclamation (!) : Happy birthday!
- parentheses ( ) : We need more RAM(Random Access Memory).
- period (.) : My name is Jenny.
- question mark(?) : How many books did you read this year?
- quotation marks(" ") : Annie said, "I like to read books."
- semicolon(;) : The teacher made her decision; moreover, the student agreed.

Illustrator Task Sheet

Name ______________________

Date ______________________

Other Group Members

____

____

Book Title

____

TasK : Draw a picture relating to the story.
You can illustrate characters, the setting, a problem, your favorite part, or a prediction of what will happen next in the story.

Summarize Task Sheet

Name ______________________________

Date ______________________________

Other Group Members

____

____

Book Title

____

TasK : Write a brief summary of the story.
Include the main events.

____

____

____

____

____

____

____

____

____

____

____

____

Word Wizard Task Sheek

Name ______________________

Date ______________________

Other Group Members

____

____

Book Title

____

Tsck : Find six interesting, powerful, or funny words from today's reading. Write the words below. Write the page number each word is on the reason you chose it. Use bookmarks to mark the pages on which the words appear in the book.

Word	Page Number	Reason for Choosing the Word

Home-Study Folder 1

MY SHAPES

MY COLORS

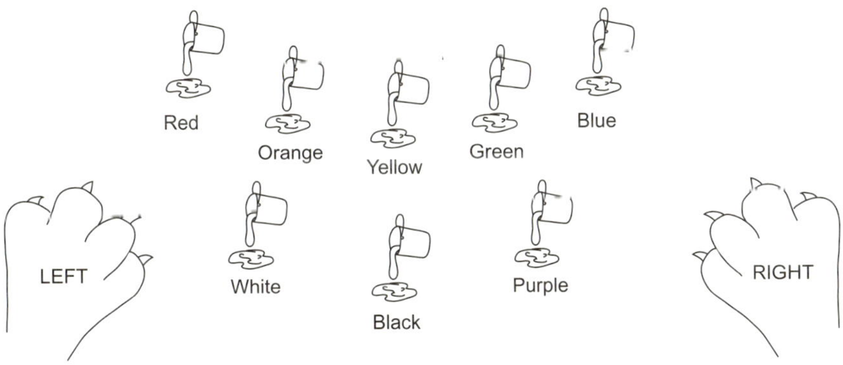

I CAN COUNT!

Name : ______________________________

Grade : ______________ Teacher : ______________

Home- Study Folder 2

Alligator

Bear

Cat

Dog

Elephant

Fish

Goat

Zebra

Horse

I CAN READ MY SIGHT WORDS!

all	and	are	an	at	be	but	came
for	form	go	got	had	have	he	her
him	his	if	in	is	it	me	of
on	one	out	said	saw	she	so	that
the	their	there	them	then	they	this	to
up	was	we	went	were	with	you	your

Yarn

Igloo

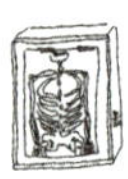
X-ray

Jet

I CAN COUNT!

1	2	3	4	5	6	7	8	9	10
11	12	13	14	15	16	17	18	19	20
21	22	23	24	25	26	27	28	29	30
31	32	33	34	35	36	37	38	39	40
41	42	43	44	45	46	47	48	49	50
51	52	53	54	55	56	57	58	59	60
61	62	63	64	65	66	67	68	69	70
71	72	73	74	75	76	77	78	79	80
81	82	83	84	85	86	87	88	89	90
91	92	93	94	95	96	97	98	99	100

Wagon

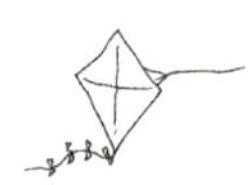
Kite

Vacuum

Lion

Umbrella

Monkey

Tent

Snake

Robot

Queen

Pig

Octopus

Nest

Modern Manuscript Alphabet

Aa *Bb* *Cc* *Dd*

Ee *Ff* *Gg* *Hh*

Ii *Jj* *Kk* *Ll*

Mm *Nn* *Oo* *Pp*

Qq *Rr* *Ss* *Tt*

Uu *Vv* *Ww* *Xx*

Yy *Zz*

참고 문헌-읽기, 쓰기

01 참고문헌- 읽기(Reading)

Allyson Daley	「Partner Reading A Way to Help All Readers Grow」	Scholastic	(2005)
Alyse Sweeney	「Teaching the Essentials of READING With Picture Books」	Scholastic	(2004)
Alice Boynton and Wiley Blevins	「Teaching Students to Read Nonfiction」	Scholastic	(2003)
American Education Publishing	「Total Reading」	School Specialty Publishing	(2005)
Antoinette Cerulli Fornshell	「Best Practices for Planning Reading & Writing Instruction」	Scholastic	(2006)
Beatrice S. Mikulecky Linda Jeffries	「More Reading Power」	Longman	(2004)
Beatrice S. Mikulecky	「Reading Power」	Longman	(2005)
Bette S. Bergeron and Melody Bradbury-Wolff	「Teaching Reading Strategies in the Primary Grades」	Scholastic	(2002)
Beverly Tyner and Sharon E. Green	「Small-Group Reading Instruction」	International Reading ociation	(2006)
Carolyn Chapman and Rita King	「Differentiated Instructional Strategies for Reading」	Corwin Press	(2003)
Carleen DaCruz Payne	「Shared Reading for Today's Classroom」	Scholastic	(2005)
Charlene M.Nichols	「Evidence-Based Reading Instruction」	International Reading ociation	(2002)
Dede Dodds, M. S. Ed. & Traci Clausen, M. S. Ed.	「Full Color Literacy Centers for Reading Skills」	Teacher Creted Materials	(2005)
Dorothy P. Hall and Cece Tillman	「Book Club Groups: A Multi level Four-Blocks Reading Strategy」	Carson-Dellosa Publishing	(2004)
Edward Fry, Ph. D.	「How to Teach Reading for Teachers, Parents, and Tutors」	Teacher Created Resources	(2006)

Evangelyn Visser and Gary M. Hanggi M. A.	「*Guided Reading in a Balanced Program*」	Teacher Created Materials	(2003)
Gail Saunders-Smith	「*The Ultimate Guided Reading How-To Book*」	Zephyr Press	(2003)
Harcourt Achieve	「*101Ways To Make Your Students Better Decoders and Readers*」	Rigby Best Teachers Press	(2006)
Holly Fitzgerald	「*Reading Skills*」	Instructional Fair	(1992)
Jennifer Overend Prior, Ph. D.	「*Reading First Activities*」	Teacher Creted Materials	(2004)
Jill and Charles Hadfield	「*Reading Games*」	Langman	(1995)
Jill Norris	「*Reading Practice at Home*」	Evan-Moor	(2000)
Jill Frankel Hauser	「*Wow! I'm Reading!*」	Williamson Publishing pany	(2000)
Joyce Graham Baltas and Denise Nessel	「*Easy Strategies and Lessons That Build Content Area Reading Skills*」	Scholastic	(1999)
Joanne Lee	「*Phonics in Reading*」	JYbooks	(2006)
Jodene Lynn Smith, M. A.	「*Reading First Activities*」	Teacher Created Materials	(2004)
Judith Mitchell and D. Ray Reutzel	「*The Reading Teacher*」	International Reading ociation	(2007)
Liane B. Onish	「*Reading Skills Card Games Long & Short Vowels*」	Scholastic	(2004)
Linda De Geronimo and Anne Diehl	「*First-Rate Reading*」	Carson-Dellosa	(2004)
Lucy McCormick Calkins	「*The Art of Teaching Reading*」	Addison Wesley Longman	(2001)
Mary Browning Schulman	「*Guided Reading in Grades 3-6*」	Scholastic	(2006)
Maureen McLaughlin Leslie Fisher	「*Research-Based Reading Lessons for K-3*」	Scholastic	(2005)

Mary Browning Schulman and Carleen Dacruz Payne	「*Guided Reading: Making It Work*」	Scholastic	(2000)
Marjorie R. Nelsen and Jan Nelsen-Parish	「*Peak With Books An Early Childhood Resource for Balanced teracy Third Edition*」	Delmar Thomson Learning	(2002)
Marilee Robin	「*Reading Activities*」	Publications International	(2001)
Mary Browning Schulman and Carleen Dacruz Payne	「*Guided Reading : Making It Work* 」	Scholastic	(2000)
Marilee Robin Burton Beth Alley Wise Suzanne I. Barchers, Ed. D.	「*Reading Activities*」	Publications InternationalLtd.	(2001)
Maureen McLaughlin, Amy Homeyer, Jennifer Sassaman	「*Research-Based Reading Lessons*」	Scholastic	(2006)
Mary Rose	「*Reading Comprehension and fluency*」	Scholastic	(2002)
Mary Browning Schulman	「*Guided Reading in Grades 3-6*」	Scholastic	(2006)
Mary Rose	「*Reading Comprehension and fluency*」	Scholastic	(2002)
Maureen McLaughlin, Leslie Fisher	「*Research-Based Reading Lessons for K-3*」	Scholastic	(2005)
Mary Browning Schulman and Carleen Dacruz Payne	「*Guided Reading : Making It Work*」	Scholastic	(2000)
Michael F. Opitz	「*Flexible Grouping in Reading*」	Scholastic	(1998)
Nancy Padak Ed. D. and Timothy Rasinski Ph. D.	「*Fast Start for Early Readers*」	Scholastic	(2005)

Paula Moore and Anna Lyon	*「New Essentials for Teaching Reading in Pre K-2」*	Scholastic	(2005)
Patricia M. Cunningham, Dorothy P. Hall and Linda B. Gambell	*「Self-Selected Reading The Four-Blocks Way」*	Carson-Dellosa Publishing	(2002)
Phyllis Sibbing	*「The Complete Book of Reading」*	American Education	
Rosalie Franzese	*「Reading and Writing in Kindergarten」*	Scholastic	(2002)
Rebecca Deangelis Callan and Laurie Deangelis	*「Teaching Reading With Rosemary Wells Books」*	Scholastic	(2007)
Ruth Foster M.Ed.	*「Nonfiction Reading Comprehension」*	Teacher Created Materials	(2006)
Susan Lunsford	*「Teaching With Favorite Read-Alouds in Prek」*	Scholastic	(2004)
Susan Lunsford	*「Teaching With Favorite Read-Alouds in Second Grade」*	Scholastic	(2004)
Susan Lunsford	*「Teaching With Favorite Read-Alouds in First Grade」*	Scholastic	(2004)
Susan Lunsford	*「Teaching with Favorite Read-Alouds」*	Scholastic	(2004)

02 참고문헌– 쓰기(Writing)

함정현 · 오현주	「다중지능이론을 활용한 유아영어교육」	동문사	(2006)
Andrew Kaplan	*「Marvelous Math Writing Prompts」*	Scholastic	(2001)
Antoinette Cerulli Fornshell	*「Best Practices for Planning Reading & Writing Instruction」*	Scholastic	(2006)
Barbara Adams	*「Scholastic Success With Writing」*	Scholastic	(2002)
Catherine M. Tamblyn	*「Our Country Write & Read Books」*	Scholastic	(2006)
Cheryl M. Sigmon and Sylvia M. Ford	*「Writing Mini-Lessons for Third Grade」*	Carson-Dellosa Publishing	(2002)
Cheryl M. Sigmon and Sylvia M. Ford	*「Just-Right Writing Mini-Lessons」*	Scholastic	(2006)
Christina L. Shahan and Donna Spencer-Verdon	*「Learning Through Movement Children's Literature」*	Teacher Created Materials	(2000)
Christy Hale	*「Collaborative Art & Writing Projects for young Learners」*	Scholastic	(2006)
Connie S. Martin	*「Trait-Based Writing Skills」*	Carson-Dellosa Publishing	(2003)
Dorothy P. Hall Patricia M. Cunningham, and Denise B. Boger	*「Writing Mini-Lessons for First Grade」*	Carson-Dellosa Publishing	(2002)
Dorothy P. Hall Patricia M. Cunningham, and Debra Renner Smith	*「Writing Mini-Lessons for Second Grade」*	Carson-Dellosa Publishing	(2002)
Dorothy S. Strickland, Richard F. Abrahamson, Roger C. Farr, Nancy R. McGee, Nancy L. Roser, Karen S. Kutiper, Patricia Smith	*「Introduction to Journal Writing」*	Steck-Vaughn Company	(1999)

Dorothy P. Hall and Patricia M. Cunningham	「*Month-By-Month Reading and Writing*」	Carson-Dellosa	(1997)
Elizabeth Suarez Aguerre	「*Classroom Literature Circles for Primary Grades*」	Carson-Dellosa Publishing	(2006)
Elizabeth Suarez Aguerre	「*Fluency Vocabulary and Comprehension*」	Carson-Dellosa Publishing	(2005)
Elizabeth Suarez Aguerre	「*Early Childhood Literacy Centers*」	Teacher Creted Materials	(2003)
George Stern	「*Writing in English*」	Didax	(2004)
Gloria Rothstein	「*Real-Life Writing Activities Based on Favorite Picture Books*」	Scholastic	(2002)
Imogene Forte	「*Ready to Learn Words & Vocabulary*」	Incentive Publications	(2003)
Jacqueline E. Kress	「*The ESL Teacher's Book of Lists*」	Jessy-Bass	(1993)
J. M. Wolf	「*Journal Activities That Sharpen Students' Writing*」	Scholastic	(2005)
Jackie Carpas and Melissa Hughes	「*Learning through Literature*」	Carson-Dellosa	(2004)
Jan Burda	「*Young Writers*」	Teacher Created Materials	(2002)
Jean Feldman	「*Reading &Writing*」	Scholastic	(2005)
Jinyoung Kim	「*Smart Writing with Grammar*」	Happy House	(2006)
Jo Fitzpatrick	「*Winter Rebus Writing*」	Creative Teaching Press	(2004)
Jo Fitzpatrick	「*Fall Rebus Writing Combining Pictures and Print to Support Beginning Writers*」	Creative Teaching Press	(2004)
Jo Ellen Moore	「*Revised Daily Language Review*」	Evan-Moor	(2005)
Judith S. Gould and Evan Jay Gould	「*Four Square Writing Method*」	Teaching & Learning ompany	(1999)
Kathleen Knoblock	「*Sight Word Comprehension Word Endings In Context*」	Bryan House	(2001)

Karen Kellaher	「*Building Skills in Writing Responding to Literature*」	Scholastic	(2002)
Karen King	「*Writing Workshop Lessons and Activities for the Writing Process*」	Teacher Created Materials	(2001)
Kathleen Hurni-Dove	「*Teaching the Craft of Writing Revising & Editing*」	Scholastic	(2006)
Linda Milliken	「*Fun with Paragraph Writing*」	Edupress	(2002)
Lola M. Schaefer	「*Teaching Young Writers: Strategies That Work*」	Scholastic	(2001)
Lucia Capacchione	「*The Creative Journal for Children* 」	Shambhala	(1982)
Mariam Jean Dreher, Kathryn A. Davis, Priscilla Waynant, Suzanne F. Clewell	「*Easy Steps to Writing Fantastic Research Reports*」	Scholastic	(2000)
Mary Rosenberg	「*Time for Kids Traits of Good Writing*」	Teacher Created Materials	(2003)
Mary Rose	「*15 Easy Lessons That Build Basic Writing Skills in Grades K-2*」	Scholastic	(2001)
Marjorie R. Nelsen, Jan Nelsen-Parish	「*Peak With Books An Early Childhood Resource for Balanced Literacy Third Edition*」	Delmar Thomson Learning	(2002)
Mariam Jean Dreher, Kathryn A. Davis, Priscilla Waynant, Suzanne F. Clewell	「*Easy Steps to Writing Fantastic Research Reports*」	Scholastic	(2000)
Michael Gravois	「*35 Ready-To-Go Ways to Publish Students' Research and Writing*」	Scholastic	(1998)
Patricia M. Cunningham and Dorothy P. Hall	「*Reading /Writing Simple Rhymes*」	Carson-Dellosa	(2003)
Patricia M.Cunningham, James W. Cunningham, Dorothy P. Hall and Sharon Arthur Moore	「*Writing the Four-Blocks Way*」	Carson-Dellosa Publishing	(2005)

Rosanne Kurstedt and Maria Koutras	「*Teaching Writing With Picture Books as Models*」	Scholastic	(2000)
Sandra Kelley	「*Spectrum Writing*」	Frank Schaffer Publications	(2003)
Susan M. Ketch and Katherine Scraper	「*Early Readers and Writers*」	Carson-Dellosa Publishing	(2005)
Susan Lunsford	「*Literature Based Mini Lessons to Teach Writing*」	Scholastic	(1998)
Sue Lewis and Rozanne Lanczak Williams	「*Writing Center Prompts Shape Stationery with Writing Prompts and Story Starters*」	Creative Teaching Press	(2001)
Susan Lunsford	「*Literature Based Mini Lessons to Teach Writing*」	Scholastic	(1998)
Veronica Robillard	「*15 Reproducible Write-and-Read Books*」	Scholastic	(1997)

▣ 저자 소개 ▣

▣ 함정현

〈학력 및 경력〉

- 하버드대학교 정치학 석사
- 브리지포트대학교 교육학 석사 · 박사
- 현재, 한서대학교 교직과 조교수
- 브리지포트대학교 교수
- 숙명여자대학교 YL-TESOL 교수
- 한서대학교 영재교육개발연구소 소장
- 한국 다중지능학회 이사
- 한국 유아특수교육학회 이사
- 경기도 파주 영어마을 교육프로그램 고문
- 부산교육청 영어수학몰입 교과서 & 교사용지도서 개발 및 소프트웨어 프로그램 개발
- ebse방송 고정출연

〈저서 및 논문〉

다중지능을 활용한 유아영어교육(동문사) 집필
미국엄마들이 아이에게 맨 처음 들려주는 영어동요 32(삼성출판사) 집필
수학이머전 교과서집필 (부산교육청)

▣ 오현주

〈학력 및 경력〉

한양대 영어영문학과 졸업
(주)대교 영어연구원 역임
한서대학교 영어지도사과정 출강
서산태안초등교사 TESOL 출강
태안군청 여성사회교육 「마더구즈(Mothergoose)」 출강

〈저서 및 논문〉

다중지능을 활용한 유아영어교육(동문사) 집필
미국엄마들이 아이에게 맨 처음 들려주는 영어동요 32(삼성출판사) 집필
수학이머전 교과서집필 (부산교육청)

Balanced Approach를 활용한

21세기 초등영어 지도방법

초판 인쇄 2009년 1월 10일
초판 발행 2009년 1월 15일

저 자 함정현 · 오현주
발행자 김 현 태
발행처 태영출판사

주 소 (157-705) 서울 구로구 구로동 104-10 동남오피스텔 201호
전 화 02-839-3757 839-3752
팩 스 02-837-3754
등 록 2005. 5. 30. 제 12-421호
E-mail tys2005@paran.com

ISBN 978-89-6302-002-0 93370
값 15000원